NINJA

SPIRIT OF THE SHADOW WARRIOR

by
Stephen K. Hayes

Edited by Bill Griffeth

Graphic Design by Walter Rickell

Library of Congress Catalog Card Number: 80-84678
ISBN No. 0-89750-073-3

Third Printing 1981

OHARA **PUBLICATIONS, INCORPORATED**
BURBANK, CALIFORNIA

DEDICATION

*This book is lovingly dedicated to
Rumiko, Duncan, Paula, Katherine, Bunny
and all my Tokyo family
for caring enough to assist me in realizing
that the ninja's heart
was intended to be a palace
and not a fortress.*

ACKNOWLEDGEMENT

I would like to express my gratitude and admiration for my teacher and mentor, Dr. Masaaki Hatsumi, 34th grandmaster of the Togakure Ryu ninjutsu tradition. While others preserve the martial methods of Japan as lifeless antiques, and yet others distort the ways to create frivolous contests, Dr. Hatsumi works to perpetuate the vitality and pragmatism of the ancient combat teachings. The art of ninjutsu that he continues to enliven is a method for enhancing the qualities of love, wonder, control, understanding and power inherent in every human being. Dr. Hatsumi is a rare combination of sincerity, relaxed humility, humor, strength, and he has the capacity to care for others. I am happy to have been able to share a part of this lifetime with him.

AUTHOR'S PREFACE

After spending eight years as a student of the Oriental fighting art of karate, a series of what I then referred to as coincidences and accidents led me to being accepted as a student of the mystical art of Japan's ninja, and to becoming the first non-Japanese ever awarded the title *Shidoshi,* or "teacher of the warrior ways of enlightenment," in the 34-generation history of the Togakure Ryu ninjutsu tradition. The road to that honor was paved with a lot of surprising discoveries about myself, the nature of combat and its part in the scheme of things, and the greater realities of the power of the individual human being.

Although I consider myself and my views to be rathei down to earth, I have witnessed and personally experienced phenomena of what appeared to be a non-physical nature, during my years of ninja training. However, further intense study brought me to the realization that all things are physical, if we are only broad-minded enough to acknowledge the fact.

This book is my way of sharing some of the ninjutsu teachings that I was fortunate enough to encounter. It is offered as an encouragement to those who are less than satisfied with safe explanations and reasonable limitations.

INTRODUCTION

Enshrouded in the antiquity of history, the true story of Japan's fabled ninja is subject to several differing interpretations today. Japanese television serials, movies and comic books continue to propagate the mythical nature of the ninja, presenting tales of superhumans who could engage occult powers to accomplish their desires. In the Western world, the few English language exposures of the ninja legend have concentrated on the military and espionage aspects of the total story, portraying the ways of ninjutsu merely as martial arts and ignoring the original spiritual nature of the people who were forced by history to become the warrior wizards of feudal Japan.

The true story of the ninja is an inspiration for us all in contemporary society. In today's crowded cities and impersonal institutions, where computerized figures keep track of our personal lives, and corporations, governments, and labor unions seem to be assuming more and more responsibility for determining our daily lifestyles, it is an exciting reassurance to encounter the fresh timelessness of the ninja way of life. From the knowledge of the ninja, we can derive our own concepts of personal power and control over the quality of our lives. We can rise above the feelings of helplessness. We can discover techniques for opening our consciousness and attuning our actions to the truth in our hearts. We can re-acquaint ourselves with the harmony inherent in the way all things unfold. We can become enlightened to the reality that happiness, joy and personal fulfillment are the birthrights of every individual.

CONTENTS

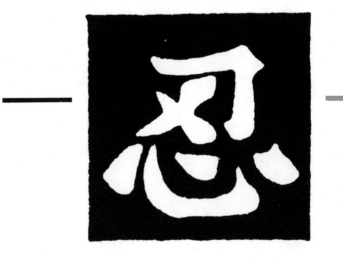

CHAPTER 1

HISTORICAL PERSPECTIVES:
The art of ninjutsu.

This is one way to be invisible:
To simply become a small part of the night
*   moving with the winds and shadows,*
*   doing what must be done,*
*   completely void of emotions,*
*   so that no one's mind can feel you,*
*   no one's heart can hear you.*

Japanese martial arts have enjoyed a popularity boom in the Western World since the end of World War II. Though the fighting sports of Japan are thought to be closely tied to the traditional culture of the island nation, it is interesting to note that judo, karate and aikido were all introduced to the Japanese only within the past century. The lesser-known art of ninjutsu, however, traces its roots back over a thousand years. The mysterious art of invisibility remains only as a legend in the minds of many Japanese today, and the teachings of this esoteric system are guarded by the few remaining masters qualified to pass on the heritage of the ninja warrior wizards.

The art of ninjutsu was developed as a military specialization by the mountain mystics of the Iga and Koga regions of Japan. Totally-developed physical bodies, calm enlightened minds and free-working spiritual powers which we would call psychic abilities today, were combined in the ninja espionage agent or guerrilla fighter. The art was made up of techniques for the prevention of danger, and included methods of physical combat, intelligence gathering and psychological warfare, and the development of occult powers.

The history of the art is closely tied to the history of the nation in which it developed. Centuries ago, in the wooded mountainous regions of south central Japan, there dwelled a collection of family clans who had dedicated themselves to seeking enlightenment through pragmatic mysticism. The teachings that constituted the core of all they studied came to them from T'ang China, having originated in the Tantric lore of far-off Tibet. As mystics, they examined the examples provided by nature to gain an understanding of their role in the phenomena of the everyday world and the universe beyond. Their goal was individual enlightenment, a consciousness of the cosmic, and an ability to work within the scheme of totality. They were content to live with nature in their mountain homes, away from the turmoil of civilization.

Total enlightenment, of course, tends to point out the discrepancies and imbalances that exist in the common view of the world, and it often occurs that those who are enlightened are misunderstood or feared by those persons lacking enlightenment. And so these families had to consider survival as part of their personal development, and ninjutsu was forced to take on martial emphasis as the necessity for protection against danger grew.

As was also true in the histories of other nations, the powers controlling the state religion did not accept the theory that anything beyond the mortal flesh could be experienced directly by anything less than a priest of the ruler's religion. The priests in counsel to the emperor did not react favorably to the tales of mystics in the mountains who had supposedly discovered methods of channeling natural forces for their own benefit. Troops were deployed to eliminate the troublemakers, and the resulting centuries-long struggle produced the legend of the supernatural ninja warriors of Japan.

As the centuries of Japanese history continued to unfold, the ninja families became more and more involved in their reputations as military specialists, and less attached to the original mystical understanding that their ancestors fought to protect. The increased demand for ninja agents, resulting from the increased activity of the Japanese war lords, required a training system that could produce espionage or combat specialists in the shortest amount of time. Physical tricks came to replace the developed natural abilities of the original ninja warriors. Systems of combat skills based on the deception of the senses became the ninja's stock-in-trade, and the invisible warriors, once motivated by love for their families, came to be feared for the ruthlessness of their determination.

As a profession, ninjutsu drew on two primary bodies of knowledge as a basis for its teachings:

Hei-ho or "combat strategy" to the greater degree

Bu-jutsu or "warrior arts" to the lesser degree

From the 13th through the 17th centuries in Japan, countless ninja families operated out of a wide range of motivations and levels of sophistication. Each family or clan had its own specific requirements for status as a ninja agent. Some groups stressed physical skills. Some stressed mental alertness. Other systems stressed political contacts. The list is long and extensive. There are, however, eight fundamental areas in which all true ninja seemed to be proficient, regardless of family affiliation:

Ki-ai: Personal harmony with the total scheme of things

The ninja had himself under control, and he had the balanced personality of an enlightened individual. He was aware of his own strengths and weaknesses, and he knew how to harmonize them with the personality of his adversary in order to accomplish the desired results. He knew the most opportune moments to act and when to lie low.

Tai-jutsu: Body skills

The ninja was trained in the techniques of unarmed fighting, including strikes, throws, locks and escapes. His fighting system was a utilitarian one based on natural movements and knowledge of the human body's weak points. Body skills also included leaping, tumbling, climbing and methods of silent movement.

Ken-po: Sword method

The ninja's sword was his primary weapon, and it was usually shorter in length than the customary samurai swords of the period. Consequently, a special method of close fighting developed with the short straight blade. In addition, the ninja sword was often used for purposes other than combat clashes.

Yari-jutsu: Spear or lance fighting

Medium-range fighting was carried out with the spear, a two- or three-edged blade mounted at the end of a two- or three-meter pole. The Japanese spear was rarely thrown, and it was most often used in straight, direct thrusts between the pieces of samurai armor.

Shuriken-jutsu: Throwing blades

For long-range targets in individual combat, the ninja used small, concealed blades which he threw at the hands or face of his adversary. The ninja's throwing blades could be straight or in a variety of multi-pointed designs, and they could be used accurately at distances of up to nine meters.

Ka-jutsu: Use of fire and explosives

Useful for creating diversions, forcing evacuations, and taking out walls and doors, fire, smoke and explosives found many uses in the arsenals of the ninja families. Many ninja were skilled at preparing their own explosives from natural elements, and several of the larger ninja organizations had their own chemists to produce large quantities of explosives for their use. In a culture such as Japan, where wood, paper and rice straw were relied upon for the construction of buildings, the threat of fire was a potent one well used by ninja agents.

Yu gei: Traditional cultural arts

The ninja was familiar with the traditional entertainment arts of the time, and he was often proficient in several of the arts himself. Painting, the tea ceremony, flower arranging, playing musical instruments, telling jokes and stories, and performing Japanese dances are a few of the arts popular in the ninja's realm. Besides the personal development afforded by them, a knowledge and appreciation of the arts was often needed to fill out a character identity being assumed for espionage purposes.

Kyo Mon: Practical education

During every active day of a ninja's life, he was exposed to new and unfamiliar surroundings and experiences. His learning system had to be general enough and broad enough in scope to provide him with a means of handling any situation that came along. Much of the ninja's practical knowledge of the world could be labeled as working common sense, or "awareness." This is not the type of information contained in books or covered by conventional educational systems, and so the ninja families relied on word-of-mouth teaching and instructional experiences to pass on the knowledge of past generations.

Considered to be far below the elite samurai status with its rigid codes of honor and propriety, the ninja were free to apply the naturalist teachings of their mystical heritage. The philosophy of ninjutsu stressed the interrelated oneness of all things in the universe. Since man is not big enough to view the entire universe, the philosophy explains, the infinite number of its parts appear to man as the "ten-thousand things," or everything that seems to exist independently. To give some perspective to the view, all these things were seen in classifications of *in* and *yo,* or negative and positive manifestations such as darkness and light, heaven and earth, male and female, firmness and softness, wetness and dryness, contraction and expansion, and endless combinations of extreme polarities.

More than merely grouping opposites under a simplistic theory, the *in* and *yo* classification scheme provided an understanding to free the ninja from the limits of viewing things as right and wrong, good and bad, or fair and unfair. Any quality inherent in a thing or situation was based merely on its relationship to other manifestations of the same quality. It is sometimes difficult for Westerners to accept or even understand this lack of rigidity in what we would call morality or principles, and indeed this concept of flexibility is in direct opposition to the theories and philosophies of many contemporary martial art systems. The ninja's outlook on his purpose in life places major emphasis on the total picture. The ever-changing results are far more significant than their means of attainment alone.

The historical ninja's primary political contribution was to maintain balance and harmony in society in the most effective manner possible. If bold cavalry charges involving thousands of soldiers were considered positive aspects of warfare, secretly capturing the battle codes or the enemy commander himself was considered a negative, or gentle, balance in the war activity. What the enemy would call "deceit, cowardice and treachery," the ninja would call "strategy, cunningness and wit."

Generations ago, when the ninja families of Japan were at the height of their power, membership in the ninjutsu tradition was determined solely by birth. The highly secret and invisible structure of the organizations prevented outsiders from working their way in, and left only the offspring of the ninja themselves as possible candidates for the roles of agent or officer in the family profession.

At the head of each clan or organization presided a *jonin* director or commander-in-chief. Half philosopher, half warrior, the jonin took on the responsibility for determining to whom his ninja would lend their support. In most ninja organizations, the identity of the jonin was concealed from the ordinary agents and operatives as a security precaution. The jonin could then observe the workings of history from a viewpoint free from the bias of his expectations of others, and free from concerns of personal safety. This role was passed down within the immediate family of the original founder, generation after generation. As children of the jonin grew, they were exposed to those teachings and experiences which would develop their abilities to view the world in a philosophical manner, understand the motivations of others, and direct the operations of a widely dispersed, highly illegal, and heavily guarded organization, to which one of them would succeed as leader.

Serving directly beneath the jonin heading each ninja organization was a group of *chunin* middle men, or executive officers. These men were responsible for interpreting and carrying out the orders of the jonin. Acting as a go-between dividing the field agents from the head of the organization, the chunin ensured the anonymity of the jonin, and they prevented double-crosses or dangerous breaches of security. The chunin possessed the skills of knowing how to get things done and a familiarity with the strengths and specialties of all the ninja field agents at his disposal. Training for the role of chunin included lessons in time and logistics management and personnel motivation, as well as contemporary and unconventional methods of warfare.

At the base of the organized hierarchy were the *genin* operatives, or ninja field agents. Men and women possessing a wide range of espionage and combat skills, the genin were the ones responsible for getting the actual work accomplished. Trained from birth by their ninja families, genin inherited a legacy of total service to their unknown jonin commander, the lords to whom the jonin contracted, and to the welfare of the nation's people as a whole. The children of genin agents began their training at an early age, practicing leaping, running and balancing exercises that were disguised as children's games. As they moved into their teen years, the children began the study of combat techniques and weapons, and the psychological effects of the mental process on the body and its physical performance. In the later teen years, skills of the trade of espionage were taught, preparing the young genin for a life of service as a ninja.

The genin ninja's loose-fitting operational combat outfit was constructed of coarse black, grey or blue fabric. A jacket was tucked into trousers which were tied onto the body, and protective sleeves covered the arms and hands. Split-toed sock-like shoes provided quiet footing, and a long scarf was worn as a combination hood and mask. The outfit included several hidden pockets into which concealed weapons or pieces of armor could be slipped.

Today, it is no longer necessary for ninja families to oversee the stability of benevolent and just governments. The art of ninjutsu has returned its emphasis to the original purposes of its founding ancestors, and the system is now taught as a method of personal enlightenment and mind-body-spirit harmony. ∎

CHAPTER 2

BUILDING BLOCKS OF THE UNIVERSE: The basis for the ninja's knowledge of himself and his world.

Know that the heavens were created
  to descend into the five elemental manifestations.
One piece
  a small mirror of all others.
It is all the same.
All the same.
Each piece of existence
  is its own small universe.
Earth
Water
Fire
Air
And the potential of the great Emptiness
  are there in everything.

To know the order of the universe
  is to understand the ways of nature
  and the proclivities of man.

One important goal in the study of ninjutsu is developing an awareness of ki-ai, allowing one to come into harmony with the "scheme of totality." More simply stated, the student of ninjutsu must become a totally natural being. This system of awareness is based on a mystical knowledge of the universe, as taught centuries ago by Japanese *yamabushi* warrior mountain priests, and developed for combat by *senin* and *gyoja* warrior ascetics who wandered in the wilderness of the Kii Peninsula.

There is nothing bizarre, unreal, or imaginary implied in the mystical teachings of ninjutsu. Mysticism is simply the study of methods used in order to directly experience an awareness of natural laws and universal consciousness. By observing nature with an unbiased mind, man comes to understand his world and how he relates to it, and thereby comes to understand himself.

Stemming from Tibetan Tantric lore, the doctrine of *mikkyo,* or the "secret knowledge," teaches that all physical aspects of existence originate from the same source and can be classified in one of five primary manifestations of the elements.

Ku—"the emptiness" or the source of sub-atomic energy; the "nothing" from which all "things" take their form

Fu—"the wind" or elements in a gaseous state

Ka—"the fire" or elements in an energy-releasing state

Sui—"the water" or elements in a fluid state

Chi—"the earth" or elements in a solid state

As a way of visualizing the creation of the universe, it is taught that ku, the emptiness, became charged with polarities that later transformed themselves into different grades of electromagnetic charge. These charges formed atoms which brought about the chemical gases of the fu state, which blended with each other to produce reactions at the ka level. Following this, the molecules became the vapor of the sui state, and later solidified to bring about the solid matter of the chi level. This progression is referred to as the descending development of the elements. To study man's relation to the rest of the universe—physically, emotionally, intellectually, or spiritually—the elemental manifestations are reversed and followed in ascending order, beginning with the chi solidity that is perhaps the simplest level with which to identify.

Combinations of atoms, with their nuclei and orbiting particles, have been viewed as models of the universe, with its whirling solar systems and galaxies. In the same manner, the human body can be seen as a miniature model of nature. Therefore, by studying the relationships of these elemental manifestations in nature, the ninja learns how to become a more natural and balanced being, more conscious of personal power and responsibilities in the stream of life.

In the human body, chi, the earth, corresponds to the bones, teeth, muscles, and other solid body tissues. Sui, the water, represents the body fluids, and those aspects of the body that provide suppleness and flexibility. Ka, the fire, is seen as the process of metabolism, and is experienced as body warmth. Fu, the wind, corresponds to the breathing cycle; the movement of air into the body and then out and into the breathing cycles of others. Ku, the emptiness, manifests itself as noise, speech, and the ability to communicate.

The physical elements of the body reverse their order of manifestation as they disappear during the process of death. Upon dying, the first element to go is consciousness of and ability to communicate with others. The breathing is the next function to cease. The next elemental manifestation to fade away is the fire, as the dead body loses its warmth. Eventually the water element falls away, and the body becomes stiff and dried out. Finally even the earth element is consumed, and the bones and teeth turn to dust or stone.

The five elemental manifestations that appear as physical matter around us are also paralleled in the stages of elevation of the personality within us. We all move up and down from one element of influence to another, and refer to the effects of our changing consciousness as our "moods."

At the earth level, the basest of the elemental manifestations, we are conscious of our own solid physicalness and stability. There is a resistance to any change or movement, and a desire to maintain things exactly as they are. Rocks are perhaps the most characteristic example of the earth principle, in that they are incapable of growth, movement, or change without the aid of the other elements. When our personality is under the influence of the earth element of manifestation, we are concerned with keeping things in their places, and we are conscious of the solid parts of the body. Chi, the earth element, has its center at the base of the spine, and the color red is associated with this physical influence.

At the water level of our physical personality, the next highest of the elemental manifestations, we are conscious of our own emotions and the fluid elements of the body. This level of consciousness is characterized by reactions to physical changes and a fluid adaptability to one's surroundings. Plants provide the clearest example of the water principle in action, in that plants are capable of independent movement and growth, they react to stimuli, and yet they are incapable of controlling their environment. When our personality is under the influence of the water element of manifestation, we react to what we encounter, and we are oriented toward the heavier emotions. Sui, the fluid element, has its center in the lower abdomen, and the color orange is associated with this emotional influence.

At the fire level, the third highest of the elemental manifestations, we are conscious of our aggressive nature. Aggression in this sense refers to dynamic or expansive energy, and it is not intended to carry a negative or violent sense. At this level of consciousness, we experience feelings of warmth, enjoyment, and direct control over our environment. Wild animals are perhaps the most characteristic example of the fire principle, in that they are capable of remembering and thinking, exerting control over their lives, and seeking pleasure. When our personality is under the influence of the fire element of manifestation, we are aware of our expansiveness, dynamic power, and our reasoning faculties. Ka, the fire element, has its center at the lower tip of the breast bone, and the color yellow is associated with this expansive, aggressive influence.

At the wind level of our personality, the fourth developmental state from base physicalness, we are aware of our own intellect and benevolence, and this influence manifests itself as feelings of wisdom and love. Human beings are the highest example of the wind principle, in that they are capable of contemplation, intellectual understanding, and love. When our personality is under the influence of the wind element of manifestation, we experience compassion, acceptance, and conscious consideration of our interactions with other individuals. Fu, the wind element, has its center in the middle of the chest, and the color green affects this benevolent influence.

The highest and most refined of the physical elements is ku, the "great emptiness of potential." Originally translated by Western scholars as "etherial substance," this emptiness is today best represented by the concept of subatomic structure. Invisible bits of energy form atoms which then combine to form the entire range of material things in existence. In the personality, the emptiness brings about the creative capability and the ability to direct the potential to become any of the four lower elemental manifestations. Ku, the source of all elements, is centered in the throat, and the color blue is associated with this creative influence.

Perhaps the most effective way to understand the influence of the various body centers of consciousness is to consider some examples of contemporary everyday experiences.

EXAMPLE ONE

You are at a ball game or crowded public park. Some distance from you, a group of drunks are carrying on. They are in their own world, having fun. Even though they are a bit noisy, they are not physically interfering with or harming anyone. From the different centers of influence, typical responses might be:

Earth	You endure. You do not even notice the drunks, or you tune them out of your consciousness and ignore them. It does not affect you.
Water	You react. You find them offensive to you and confront them, call the authorities, or get up and go somewhere else. It is annoying.
Fire	You enjoy. You find them amusing. You watch the "street show" and see humor in the total picture—the actions of the drunks, the reactions of the people around them. It is hilarious.
Wind	You contemplate. You feel good because they are enjoying themselves, but you are concerned that they might harm themselves or make others uncomfortable. With a smile, you wonder to yourself why some people have to get drunk before they can enjoy life with child-like abandon. It is touching.

EXAMPLE TWO

You have won the Irish Sweepstakes. Under the influence of the different elemental levels, your reactions might be:

Earth	You pay off all of your debts and put the money in the bank. It does not affect your lifestyle.
Water	You quit your job to travel, and do all the things you have always wanted to experience.
Fire	You build a dream house, and turn your hobby into a business.
Wind	You set up trust funds for your family, and invest the rest of the money where it will be of benefit to society.

EXAMPLE THREE

You are caught in a traffic jam on the freeway. The cars are inching along bumper-to-bumper under the summer skies. From the different centers, typical response might be:

Earth	You endure. You are aware of time being wasted and you realize that there is nothing that you can do about it. You ride out the inevitable slow flow, and let your mind wander or listen to the radio as a diversion.
Water	You react. You find the traffic jam angering and annoying. You formulate an alternate route plan and look for a way out. You change lanes back and forth to fill up gaps in the traffic, or drive along the shoulder past sitting vehicles. You leave the freeway if possible, and use smaller local roads to get to your destination.
Fire	You enjoy. You realize that jams like this are a natural part of daily driving and so you make the best of it. You try to get some sun on your face through the open roof of your car. You talk with the driver of the car next to you. You turn sideways so that you can see and converse with your passengers. You make up mental games for youself, like picking out the worst and best looking vehicles on the road, the most attractive male and female in sight, etc. You check out the landscape around you, noting new sights in familiar territory.
Wind	You contemplate. You feel that the jam is unfortunate, because it is interfering with so many people's day. You wonder what the cause is, and you fear that perhaps someone has been injured or is in trouble. You work to keep the traffic flowing as best you can—pausing to let others into the flow, speeding up to fill gaps so others behind you will not have to brake. You think about ways to improve the situation for all and ways to avoid these jams in the future.

EXAMPLE FOUR

You are deciding which film to see. The strengths of the various centers might prompt you to select:

Earth	A documentary, or war story
Water	An erotic film, or an adventure
Fire	A comedy, or musical
Wind	A love story, or drama

EXAMPLE FIVE

Your primary outlook on why you work at your particular job reflects one center of influence:

Earth	You have to make a living in order to have food and shelter.
Water	It is a means to having a lot of money, and all the possessions and experiences you want.
Fire	You enjoy the activity so much that you cannot imagine doing anything else, regardless of remuneration.
Wind	You feel that your role is to serve others and better your world, and your job is your contribution.

EXAMPLE SIX

You are by yourself at night, eating at a small roadside diner. A couple of obnoxious tough guys spot you and sit down across the table from you. Their talk is derisive and decidedly threatening. Though they have not yet physically interfered with you, it is obvious that they intend to rough you up. Through the influence of the various centers, your behavior might be:

Earth	You continue to eat in an undisturbed fashion. You pay only slight attention to the comments, but you do not acknowledge the threatening nature of the talk or let it bother you. You follow normal routine in a quiet, confident manner while checking out the locations of doors and anything that could aid you when the fight begins. You finish the meal, pay the bill, and walk out if you can. You use your coolness as a possible deterrent and let them make the first move if there is to be any physical encounter.

Water	You joke around with them and make laughing wisecracks as though you were one of their buddies. You take over and direct the conversation whenever you get the chance. You ask them where you should go to find some entertainment, ask them about their cars or motorcycles. You sound naively sincere and you seem to be convinced that they will not really hurt you. You laugh it off when they make direct reference to injuring you. You suddenly tell them you will be right back and take off for the restroom. When they amble in to find you, you surprise attack with a trash can battering ram to the face, and finish them off with any weapons or aids you can improvise. You disappear before they regain consciousness.
Fire	When it is obvious that they are about to make their move, you dramatically lift the pepper shaker to a position about two feet above the table top. You stare them in the eye and then shift your vision to the raised pepper shaker, taking their eyes with you. With their attention on your hands, you slowly and deliberately remove the shaker cap. While they are watching your show, you inconspicuously raise one foot beneath the table and position the heel in front of the crotch of the man across from you. With the cap off the pepper shaker, you suddenly roar with an explosive shout and fling the pepper into the second man's face, and immediately shove the heel of your poised foot into the crotch of the thug across from you. You dump the table over on them both, while kicking and beating them into submission. You disappear before any shocked witnesses can react or call the police.
Wind	You begin acting crazier than they are. You twitch around and make incoherent references to keeping a low profile for awhile so the police will not find you. You giggle a lot and then fly into a rage over something insignificant. You go into some sort of fit or seizure, and your attackers slip away to avoid the attention you are drawing.

EXAMPLE SEVEN

Your primary reason for taking up golf or tennis is a result of one of the following centers being in prominence:

Earth	Physical fitness and health benefits
Water	Social benefits
Fire	Challenge of competition
Wind	It gives you a sense of uplifting freedom

EXAMPLE EIGHT

You find yourself involved in a discussion of personal, religious concepts. All sorts of different and new ideas are being expressed by the participants. From the different levels of personality consciousness, your reaction might be:

Earth	You hold your ground. Despite anything that is said, you do not alter your personal beliefs. You feel no need to defend your views or even consider the views of your discussion partners.
Water	You respond to the challenge. You defend your own position and use questions to weaken the solidity of conflicting viewpoints. You find yourself highly annoyed (or completely converted) at the close of the discussion.
Fire	You consider it a learning experience. You ask a lot of questions and consider your own views in light of the answers you receive. You look for weaknesses or discrepancies in your beliefs and use the discussion to become clearer on your own thoughts.
Wind	You interact to encourage others. You relate your personal experiences as answers to questions posed by your discussion partners. You leave the others with suitable questions that you feel will benefit them as they determine their own answers.

EXAMPLE NINE

A close friend is going through a divorce. From the various centers of influence, your assistance could take one of the following forms:

Earth	You encourage your friend to do everything to end up with as much of the mutual property and income as possible.
Water	You back your friend in creating the public impression that the divorce was the responsibility of your friend's spouse.
Fire	You get your friend out into social activity as a single person.
Wind	You console your friend with the fact that divorce simply legally ends a marrage that has already completely fulfilled its purpose.

It should be stressed that no one element of influence is inherently better or worse than another. In fact, one of the greater reasons for studying the effects of the influence centers is to realize the impossibility of assigning arbitrary value judgment labels to our experiences. Every emotion in the wide range of moods available to the human being can be seen as more or less appropriate in any given set of circumstances.

There are, however, those times when a particular emotion may be regarded as negative or positive based on its effectiveness in the given situation. In the following example, a positive manifestation (effective approach to the situation) and a negative manifestation (ineffective approach to the situation) for each level of consciousness are illustrated. Appropriateness in the situation is not only determined by one's mood (element of influence), but also by the manner chosen to express the mood.

EXAMPLE TEN

Your mate dies. Your resultant behavior could be governed by the centers of influence in one of the following ways:

The positive manifestation of the *earth* center is *stability.*	You comfort others who loved your mate also.
The negative manifestation of the *earth* center is *self-defeating stubbornness.*	You refuse to acknowledge the death and continue to speak and think as though your mate were still living.
The positive manifestation of the *water* center is *flexibility.*	You adopt a new lifestyle that fits your single status.
The negative manifestation of the *water* center is *immobilizing emotionalism.*	You retreat and dwell in all-consuming grief.
The positive manifestation of the *fire* center is *aggressive vitality.*	You recall happily the love and warmth that your mate shared together.
The negative manifestation of the *fire* center is *overwhelming fear.*	You feel deserted and left alone, and you are terrified of the future.
The positive manifestations of the *wind* center are *wisdom* and *love.*	You know that your partner has moved on to a new adventure, just as you and everyone else will do.
The negative manifestation of the *wind* center is *truth-obscuring intellectualization.*	You work at analyzing the circumstances, trying to determine why your mate was taken from you, or what has become of your deceased partner's spirit.

Examples of the ku, or source-level, influence could not be included in the preceding charts, because there is no set, characteristic style of behavior associated with ku level of consciousness. Ku is the creative potential of becoming whatever is appropriate for the situation and the direction of energy from one level of awareness to another as needed.

The voice is one reflection of the influence of the emptiness center, as it takes on the qualities of the four lower elemental manifestations and inspires precise, though often unconscious, responses in others. With the earth center of influence, the voice is heavy, deep, commanding and authoritarian. The lower vibrations of the sound and the gut-level quality of the tone give the chi voice a solid, grounded feeling. Under the influence of the water level of consciousness, the voice is sexy, husky or emotional. The fire level voice is warm, mirthful, and enthusiastic, with a happy aggressive tone to it. Terror or hysteria can also take the voice to the ka level of manifestation. Under the wind influence, the voice is in the higher, softer registers, and has a soothing or loving tone to it.

What vocal expression does not match the body's center of influence, confusion or suspicion develops in the listener, as the speaker's ulterior motives show through. Even in untrained individuals, an unconscious awareness sometimes produces an intuitive feeling that something is not right or out of place with the words being heard. For example, words of love influenced by the water level of personality are interpreted as lust. Words of command influenced by the water level of personality are interpreted as emotional self-interest. Words of command influenced by the wind level of personality are interpreted as weakness. Thorough understanding of the relationship of the body's influence centers and the voice gives the ninja the ability to "see through" others, and avoid arousing suspicion with his own communications.

Perhaps somewhat representative of the concept of ku consciousness reflected in personality is the physically enlightened master of one of the inwardly-directed Zen arts usually associated with the Orient. This type of individual moves through life ever-centered, firmly fixed in the present moment, and always mildly joyous with whatever or whomever he or she encounters. This person is unencumbered by the rules and belief systems that limit the chi earth consciousness. He or she is not controlled by or susceptible to the emotional reactions that cloud the sui water consciousness. This individual is not driven by the ambitions or fears that dominate the ka fire level, nor is he or she swayed by the concepts of right and wrong that appear from the intellect operating at the fu wind level of consciousness. The personality becomes so pure that there seems to be no personality there at all. These individuals are so in touch with their true natures that they become impossible to predict, and therefore impossible to control. ∎

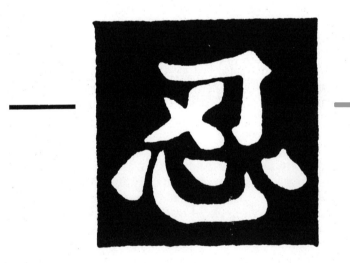

CHAPTER 3

**FIGHTING:
The mind and body
harmoniously dealing
with danger.**

The benevolent warrior
   understands the true scope and priorities
   of warfare.

He first defends his country
   the land that shelters and feeds him
   the community that houses his family.

He next defends his family alone
   the ones who turn to him for deliverance
   the people who share his love.
He lastly defends himself.

In the giving of strength to protect
   meaningful places
   and loving faces
   the ninja serves his own heart.

O ne particular mood is likely to produce more desired results under any given set of conditions. In the same manner, an appropriate fighting method is needed to prevail in any given self-defense situation. Appropriateness in a fight is based on the combined aspects of the total situation, with all details taken into account. Our surroundings, our mood, the amount of room we have, social and moral considerations, the number and size of our attackers, and the severity of their intentions are all determining factors. Unlike a sports contest, there are no agreements, weight classifications, or safety considerations.

Each fighting technique encountered in the training of Togakure Ryu ninjutsu can be classified by one of the elemental manifestations. The ninja's fighting method is taught as a total system that includes sticks, fists, blades, throws, mental outlooks, and all aspects of personal combat which might be faced. As a general guideline, the following approaches to a fighting class reflect the specific elemental manifestations of consciousness influencing the response.

From the earth level, you hold your ground solidly, taking the onslaught without letting it affect you. You know that your strength will prevail. The hips are the body's center of motion and consciousness, a familiar concept for judo players. Your adversary feels as though he is fighting against a rock—you are impervious to anything he does.

From the water level of consciousness, you shift and flow, using distancing and unexpected movement to defeat your adversary. You know that your flexibility and cleverness will win out. The lower abdomen is the body's center of motion and consciousness, a concept familiar to aikido practitioners. Your assailant feels as though he is fighting against the ocean waves—you recede from his advances and then crash back to knock him over.

From the fire level, you go after your adversary with fierce resolve. The harder he fights, the more intense your blows become. You are committed to injuring him in direct proportion to the strength he uses against you. The solar plexus is the body's center of motion and consciousness, and the total body moving into the opponent is an action familiar to karate students. Your adversary feels as though he is fighting against a brushfire—you flare up hotter and brighter the more he beats and fans that ''fire'' in an attempt to put it out.

Under the influence of the wind level of the personality, you fight with purely defensive moves, protecting yourself well without causing undue injury to your adversary. You use enough force to discourage him without harshly punishing him, and your counterattacks intercept his moves and stun him without the necessity of blocking first. The center of the chest is the body's center of motion and consciousness, allowing for the quick lightness demonstrated by boxers as they duck, slip and roll with the punches. Your attacker feels as though he is fighting against the wind—you become ever-elusive and occasionally sting his eyes with a little dust as a gentle dissuader.

Under the influence of the source level, the emptiness, you use your creative powers in thoughts, words and actions to create an environment in which you have no need to fight with anyone. An adversary never appears.

In almost all instances of conflict or competition, these primary methods of relating to one's opposition will manifest themselves. Whether it is a fistfight, an auto race, or a verbal exchange, the body centers of consciousness or tension are identical, and there are appropriate as well as inappropriate approaches to handling the situation as it unfolds from second to second. These centers of consciousness and approaches to physical self-defense are not "concentrated on" or actively pursued. They are merely ways of classifying thought and action after they have taken place. These classifications are labels for our methods of relating to ever-changing surroundings. A successful outcome will be the result of properly balancing out all aspects of the situation. Unsuccessful results develop through a lack of sensitivity or awareness of what is needed to create balance.

Corresponding to each of the elemental manifestations as reflected in defensive styles is a specific fighting pose from which the initial fighting moves may proceed. The pose itself is assumed naturally as the body goes through the realization that defensive action is needed. In this manner, each posture, or *kamae*, is a physical reflection of the mental attitude and psychological set.

The earth level of consciousness is characterized by the natural posture, or *shizen no kamae*. Just as the name implies, the *shizen* pose is a natural, relaxed standing position. The feet are planted hip-width apart, each taking an equal amount of the body weight. The knees are flexed to a straight position, neither bent forward nor locked back. The body's stability is sensed in the thighs and lower portions of the hips. The shoulders are relaxed and the arms and hands hang naturally. The eyes gaze forward with a somewhat soft, distant focus, taking in all within the frame of vision without concentrating on any one limiting point.

The body should have a somewhat heavy feel to it, as though the force of gravity were more intense than it normally is. The muscles are relaxed, and their weight is felt on the undersides. In the natural posture, the fighter appears to be firmly holding his ground, confident and unshakeable as a tree rooted in the earth.

Maintaining the natural posture may be more difficult than it sounds because grounded stability is not easily imitated. There must be a total absence of superfluous body movements, such as darting about or lowering your eyes, clenching your hands, or shifting your weight from leg to leg. It is interesting to practice the shizen pose in normal daily activity to see how much unconscious movement we carry out without thinking. As a reversed method of practice, it is enlightening to watch others in different situations as they assume varying degrees of confidence and grounded action. By watching the outward bodily manifestations of voice, movement and bearing, we can get a clear idea of how another person is thinking and relating to his surroundings.

Defensive Posture
(ichimonji no kamae)

Offensive Posture
(jumonji no kamae)

Natural Posture
(shizen no kamae)

Receiving Posture
(hira no kamae)

In self-protection situations, the natural posture is most often found being used in response to surprise attacks under circumstances that were not considered to be threatening. A conversation partner who suddenly becomes argumentative, a person attempting to take your place in a theater ticket line, or an inanimate object that threatens to move and injure are examples of this type of interaction. The shizen no kamae, with its earth stability, also conveys a feeling of control over the situation, and the power to prevent drastic violent action from taking place.

The water level of consciousness is characterized by the defensive posture, or *ichimonji no kamae*. The physical embodiment of a defensive view of combat, the ichimonji pose enables evasive, surprising movements. The body is in a low, crouched position with the trunk turned sideways toward the adversary, and the legs and knees are deeply flexed to keep the hips low. The foot position roughly forms the letter *L,* with the leading foot pointing at the attacker and the rear foot pointing in the direction in which the torso has been turned. The body trunk is held upright over the rear leg, which supports approximately 70 percent of the weight. The body's balance and potential for movement are sensed in the lower abdomen below and behind the navel. The shoulders are turned with the body trunk to line up with the adversary, and the leading hand is extended forward in a fending manner while the rear hand is poised beside the face and neck in a protective manner. The eyes are gazing along the leading shoulder and arm, taking in the total body of the attacker.

The body should have a light, responsive feel to it, and all motion should begin by moving the abdomen and allowing the body to follow. As the hips move, the feet and torso follow, preventing a loss of balance or slow, predictable movement. To assume the ichimonji posture from a natural stance, the hips are lowered back and to the side at a 45-degree angle to the anticipated attack force. As the seat moves back and down, the rear support foot shifts into position with a retreating action that drags the leading foot back slightly.

In self-protection situations, the ichimonji no kamae is best used to combat larger or more aggressive adversaries. The defensive pose and its footwork are practiced with evasive, zig-zag pattern movements that retreat to the inside and outside of the attacker's striking limbs. A low posture will keep the body in balance and facilitate fast, erratic moves, even on unlevel ground or unstable surfaces. From the safety of the defensive posture, hard-hitting blocking strikes can be applied to the attacker's incoming limbs.

The fire level of consciousness is characterized by the offensive posture, or *jumonji no kamae*. A charging, forward moving body pose, the jumonji posture is used as a base from which to launch the punches, strikes and kicks of the ninja's *taijutsu* fighting method. The body faces the adversary with one side leading and the weight distributed evenly over the two legs. The feet are roughly hip-width apart with the toes pointing inward slightly, and the knees should be flexed to give the feet a ground-gripping quality. The body's center of movement and balance is the solar plexus, the back is held straight without leaning forward or to the side, and the hips are low. The fists are held in front of the chest, and they are crossed at the wrists with the leading-side hand in front of the trailing-side hand.

The body should have a slightly tensed or potentially explosive feel to it. In the jumonji pose, the intention is to overtake or overwhelm the adversary. To move into the offensive posture from a natural stance, the leading foot shifts forward into position as the hands come up along the ribs and in front of the chest. The hips angle slightly to the side and drop as the body moves into the attacking pose, and the eyes lock onto their target. Progression forward and backward in the jumonji no kamae is carried out through short choppy steps or shuffling foot slides in a level gliding manner that prevents the body from bobbing up and down. The feet move at the same moment as the upright body trunk, keeping the shoulders from falling into the attack, and related hand actions usually accompany the footwork.

In self-protection situations, the jumonji offensive posture is best used to combat hesitant or cautious adversaries, and to add the element of surprise to a confrontation in which inevitable explosive hostility is building. From this offensive posture, initiative is taken in the fight, forcing the adversary into a defensive or retreating attitude. The intense techniques from the jumonji posture go after and take out the enemy's weapons, rather than defend against them.

The wind level of consciousness is characterized by the receiving posture, or *hira no kamae*. The receiving posture couples a solidly grounded base and the power to harmonize the body with the intentions of an attacker. The feet are placed hip-width apart and carry the body weight evenly. The knees are flexed slightly more than in the natural posture, creating a feeling of balance in the hips similar to that experienced just before sitting down on a chair. The back is straight, in a natural manner, and the shoulders are relaxed. The arms extend outstretched to the sides with the hands open, and the eyes gaze forward in soft focus, taking in the whole picture without limiting the concentration to one single point.

The body should have an extremely light, almost floating feel to it.

Epitomizing some concepts that are the opposite of those embodied in the shizen earth pose, the wind level hira no kamae prepares the fighter for adapting to and going with the attacking moves of the enemy. This adaptive sensitivity is centered in the chest behind the breastbone. The evenly distributed balance facilitates quick and easy movement in any direction in response to the attacker's intentions. The outstretched arms have the potential of becoming tools to carry out punches, strikes, deflections, blocks, throws, locks, as well as acting as distractions and calming techniques.

In self-protection situations, the hira posture is used to handle attackers in a way that subdues them without injury, if possible. The pose itself is non-threatening, and it appears to be an attempt to fend-off attack, or to reassure an adversary that there is no hostile intention, as upraised open hands traditionally symbolize surrender or benediction. From the hira no kamae, footwork proceeds with circular or straight-line movements, as appropriate for the specific circumstances. The arms are used to entangle the adversary with spiraling actions, or intercept the adversary with direct advances.

From the various fighting postures, the ninja's taijutsu self-defense techniques can be classified in two broad ranges of combat method. *Dakentaijutsu,* or technique for attacking the bones, consists of strikes, punches, kicks and blocks directed toward the attacker's bone structure. *Jutaijutsu,* or grappling technique, consists of throws, locks and chokes directed against the joints and muscles of the adversary, as well as flexible, adaptive—sometimes almost acrobatic—escapes and counters for throws, locks and strikes applied by the attacker. Unlike sports contests that limit the techniques to throwing, punching, or grappling only, actual life-protecting combat will always combine aspects from both of the two major technique classifications as distance, energy and urgency dictate.

Earth Response in the Striking Method

From the natural posture, (1) the defender observes as his adversary initiates a right-face punch. He maintains the natural posture, and (2) shifts his left side forward slightly, sending his left hand straight at the attacker's face. Then (3) he slams the base of his left palm up under the attacker's nose and allows his fingertips to strike the attacker's eyes. The defender's left elbow can deflect the at-

tacker's right forearm if necessary. Finally (4) he maintains his position and pulls straight down with his clawing left hand, catching the attacker by the lower lip and jaw. The fingernails are used to cause pain to the soft tissues of the mouth and gums and force the attacker to the ground. The entire sequence is completed in less than two seconds.

3

4

Water Response in the Striking Method

From the natural posture, (1) the defender observes as his adversary initiates a right-face punch attack. He then falls back (2) from the attacker's lunging punch, and (3) strikes his punching arm with an injurious counterblow from the defensive pose. Immediately (4) he shifts forward into the offensive posture, using his body force to propel a strike

4

through the attacker's punching arm. The hand snaps open at the point of impact, concentrating power delivery in the edge of the palm. The knife-hand strike (5&6) smashes through the punching arm, taking it out of the way and unbalancing the attacker. The entire series of moves is performed in a two-second time interval.

5

6

Fire Response
in the Striking Method

From the natural posture (1) the defender observes as his adversary initiates a right-face punch attack. He then charges forward (2&3) in the offensive posture, bringing his leading arm up beneath the attacker's lunging punch, knocking his arm to the side. Immediately (4&5) he pulls his trailing leg into position for a kicking counterattack. The defender continues his forward momentum (6&7) by slamming the base of his heel into the attacker's midsection, injuring him and knocking him backwards.

2

4

5

7

Wind Response
in the Striking Method

From the natural posture (1) the defender observes as his adversary initiates a right-face punch attack. He then pivots clockwise (2-4) while assuming the receiving pose. As he moves past the attacker (5) the defender suddenly straightens his shoulders (6) sending an open-hand slapping strike to the attacker's solar plexus. As he moves into position behind the attacker (7&8) the defender uses both hands to secure a hold on the attacker's jacket and hair. If necessary (9-11) the defender can use the bottom of his foot to fold the attacker's knee in order to force him into submission.

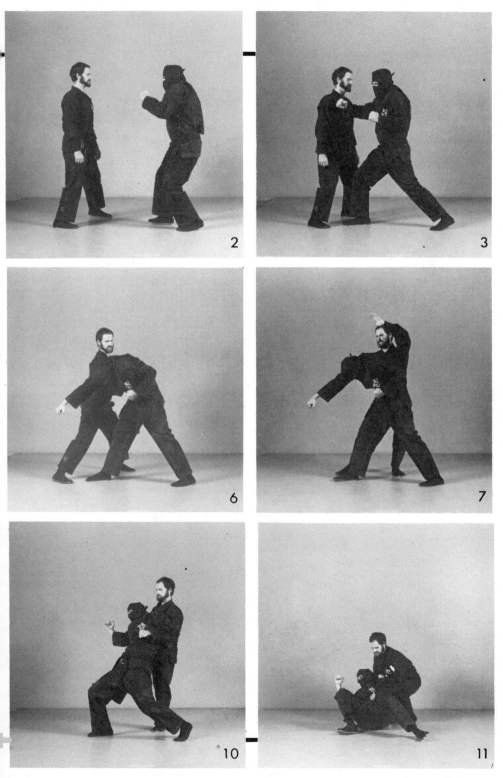

JUTAIJUTSU

Earth Response
in the Grappling Method

From the natural posture (1&2) the defender observes as his adversary grabs him in preparation for a throw. The defender maintains the natural posture (3) and brings his right hand up to cover the attacker's right hand. He then uses his curled fingers and the base of his palm (4) to apply crushing pressure to the joints of the attacker's thumb. The defender's grip compacts the natural folds of the joints, (5) producing intense pain. Finally (6-8) the attacker is forced to the ground as the defender straightens and lowers his controlling arm.

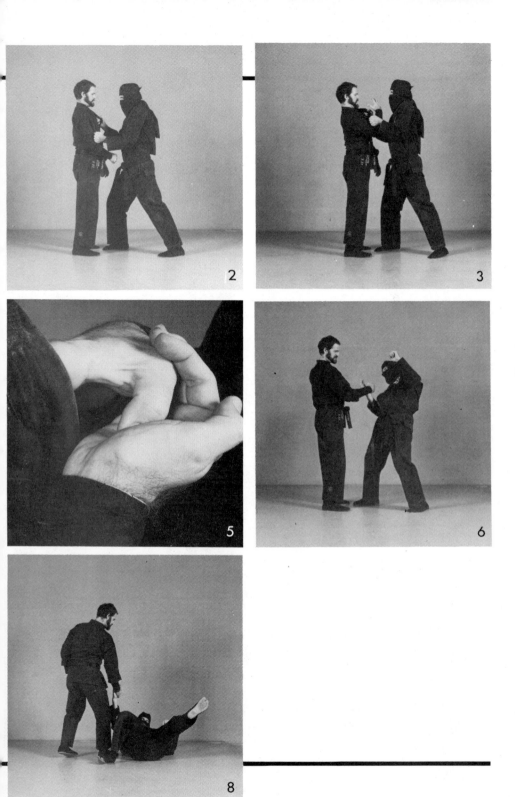

Water Response
in the Grappling Method

From the natural posture (1-3) the defender observes as his adversary grabs him in preparation for a throw. He then steps back into the defensive posture with his right foot (4&5) using his left hand to cover the attacker's right grabbing hand. He moves back further (6-9) by stepping away with his left foot, pulling the attacker to submission with an outward wrist twist.

1

4

5

8

9

1

Fire Response in the Grappling Method

From the natural posture (1&2) the defender observes as his adversary grabs him in preparation for a throw. He then charges forward (3-5) wedging the attacker's neck into a right-over-left crossed-wrist choke. As the attacker lifts and struggles to free himself (6) the defender drops into a crouch with a clockwise spin, allowing his arms to uncross naturally. The defender straightens his arms (7-10) and pushes them forward while flexing his knees and rising. The attacker is thrown forward by the combined motions, and is slammed on to his head or shoulders.

4

7

8

Wind Response in the Grappling Method

From the natural posture (1&2) the defender observes as his adversary grabs him in preparation for a throw. The attacker executes a rear-hip throw (3&4) attempting to slam the defender on to his head or back. The defender (5) goes with the throw instead of resisting. He then brings his legs over his head (6) with a speed faster than that used by the attacker in executing his throw. As he lands (7-9) the defender uses a finger pressure attack to the attacker's lower abdomen to force him to the ground.

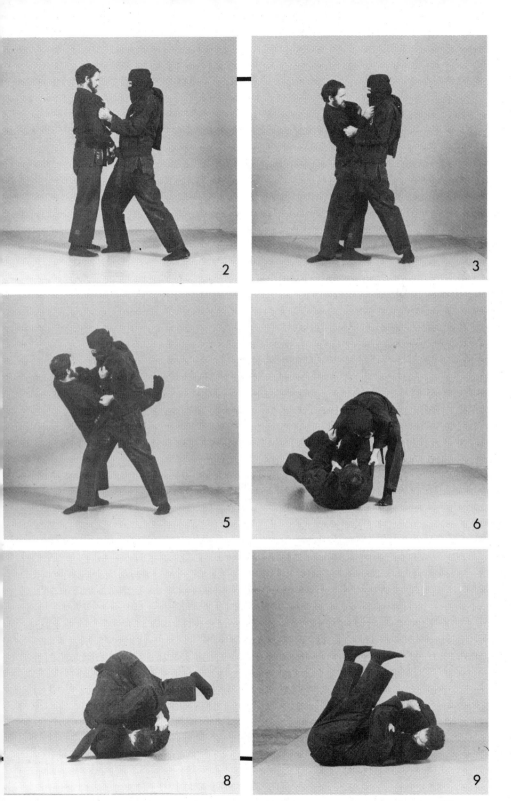

1

2

Ninja training today also involves perfecting skills with several classical combat tools. Weapon training with the historical gear enhances overall coordination, and it provides physical models from which psychological or philosophical lessons can be taught. But most important of all, it allows the student to learn the ability to recognize and improvise self-defense tools from common articles in the environment. All ninja weapons are timeless in the sense that they're fundamental combat tools rather than unique or unusual gimmicks. Sticks, blades, pieces of rope or chain can all be

Earth Response with the Long Staff

From a variation of the natural posture (1) the defender observes as the attacker initiates a short-stick clubbing attack. The defender maintains the natural pose (2) and pushes his right hand out, propelling the upper tip of his staff down and forward. The tip of the staff

3

found readily, and the fighter who is proficient in their use need not endanger himself by having to rely on carrying a specialized weapon with him at all times.

The ninja's weapon fighting methods are identical to the ninjutsu unarmed combat in terms of body dynamics and the coordination of physical response and mental observation. The fighting poses are slightly altered to accommodate the physical dimensions of the weapons, but they do follow the general classifications of purpose relating to the five elemental manifestations, just like the taijutsu postures.

4

5

(3) hits the attacker at the base of the throat, stopping his advance. The defender (4) then uses his left hand to reinforce his right, and (5) scrapes the tip of his staff down the breast bone in the center of his adversary's chest (6) driving him to the ground.

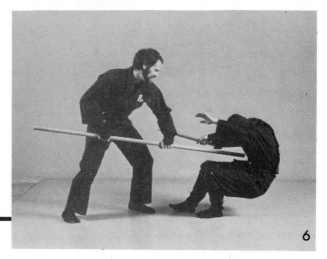

6

1

2

3

STICK FIGHTING

A natural progression from unarmed defense is the *bojutsu* stick fighting system. Traditional weapons the Japanese samurai culture, the wooden cane and staff are natural extensions of the arms, and they are relatively easy to master once unarmed fighting proficiency has been developed. The *roku-shaku-bo,* or six-foot staff, is just under two meters in length, and the

Water Response with the Short Stick

From the natural posture (1) the defender observes as his adversary initiates a right grabbing attack. The defender falls back into the defensive posture (2&3) out of the attacker's reach. As the attacker moves forward (4) with a

han-bo, or "half-staff," is a cane just under one meter in length. Contemporary students of ninjutsu find that stick techniques experienced in training are easily adaptable to real-life situations where a walking stick, yard rake, tennis racket, or even a rolled-up newspaper, can easily be found in everyday surroundings and pressed into service as defensive weapons.

4

5

second grabbing attempt, the defender shifts back and to the right to avoid the attacker's left hand. Finally, (5&6) the defender seizes the attacker's extended arm and holds him in place for a strike to the ribs with the cane.

6

BLADE WEAPONS

Ninjutsu's *ken-po* blade technique teaches practical skills with handheld as well as thrown blades. The formal training is made up of fast-draw techniques for pulling the sword or knife from the scabbard and cutting in one simultaneous movement, plus fencing skills for using the handheld blade against an attacker's

Water Response with the Ninja Sword

From a defensive sword posture (1) the defender observes as his adversary prepares to throw a star shuriken. The attacker throws the shuriken (2) at the defender's face. The defender ducks (3) and

weapon, and throwing skills for hitting distant targets with the released blade. Though the two-handed Japanese sword is used for some practice sessions in the training hall, today's student of ninjutsu could use a contemporary hunting knife, kitchen implement, or garden tool in a true life or death struggle.

deflects the shuriken star with his sword. As the shuriken star flies off harmlessly (4) the defender charges into the attacker (5&6) with a sword cut before he can throw the next star.

Fire Response with the Throwing Blade

From a variation of the offensive posture (1) the defender observes as the attacker initiates a vertical slash with a sword. As the attacker moves forward (2) the defender (3) pulls a straight shuriken throwing blade from its concealed sheath. The defender lifts the blade (4) to a throwing position beside his head (5) gripping the shuriken by its handled end. The boldness of this defensive attacking action should be enough to stop the prudent adversary from continuing his advance. If it is necessary to prevent being killed by a raging attacker (6) the blade can be thrown by snapping the arm down and pushing the shoulder forward. When the arm reaches a horizontal extended position (7) the blade is released to sail straight across the short distance into its target.

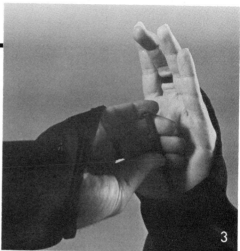

CHAINS AND CORDS

Chain and cord weapons also follow the unarmed fighting system in their practical application. The *kusarifundo,* a short small-linked chain with weighted ends, the *kyotetsu shogei,* a blade weapon attached to a three-meter cord, and the *kusarigama,* a four-meter chain attached to a long handled sickle, are three of the flexible ninja weapons that are practiced today for their

Fire Response with the Chain and Sickle

Holding the kusarigama chain and sickle in the offensive posture (1) the defender observes as the attacker initiates a horizontal slash with his sword. The attacker charges in with the cut (2) and the defender counter attacks (3) by slinging the weighted chain around the attacker's blade as it moves forward. The de-

practical application in street self-defense. Short chain techniques practiced in the training hall can be duplicated with a belt, camera strap, dish towel or necktie when self-preservation warrants it. The long cord methods can be utilized with an electrical appliance power cable, fishing tackle, water ski or mountain climbing robe, or a telephone receiver cord in an actual attack situation.

fender (4) sidesteps and pulls the chain in the direction of the attacker's cut to direct the blade away from its target. The defender then steps forward (5) moving past the attacker's right side, and he levels the sickle portion of his weapon to hit the attacker while escaping the danger of the attacker's sword.

1

By continuously examining his responses to danger and conflict, the student of ninjutsu can eventually learn what is appropriate as a response to any given situation in order to bring him what he wants. He can recognize what works and what does not work, and he can develop the intuitive

2

Wind Response with the Short Chain Fighting Method

From the natural posture, (1) the defender observes as the attacker initiates a clubbing attack with a short stick. Stretching the short chain between both hands (2&3) the defender slips to the side of the attacker's strike and brings the chain up from beneath the attacker's clubbing arm. Holding his hands above the attacker's arm as it is wedged in the "V" of the chain (4) the defender pivots with a clockwise motion, crossing the weighted ends of the chain over the attacker's

3

nature that will allow him to know the best response every time without having to think it through mechanically. The ninja warrior's approach to winning is not merely a special method of fighting. It is a total dedication to personal perfection— the achievement of harmony with the world. ∎

4

5

forearm. The chain naturally entraps the arm with this movement, and it is not necessary for the defender to wrap or loop the chain around the attacker's moving arm. The club slides harmlessly inside the defender's right arm. The defender (5) continues his clockwise spinning motion, capturing and redirecting the attacker's force. The defender (6) uses his left knee and the taut chain to bring the attacker into submission on the ground.

6

CHAPTER 4

THE SIXTH CENTER:
The brain as a tool of the spirit.

Men are helpless
only when they see themselves as helpless,
The present is our only opportunity for power.
The passage of time controls
and bends all things
only when we believe in
the passage of time.
The future lived
is merely yet another
Now.

Beyond the five manifestations of physicalness lies the second major realm of personal power—the mind and mental processes. This sixth center of consciousness is felt in the middle of the cranial cavity, and it is traditionally associated with the area of the brow between and slightly above the eyes.

In the mystical teachings of ninjutsu, the mind was seen as a bridge between pure consciousness and the body in which that consciousness temporarily resides. The mind is, in essence, an interpreting device, organizing or translating all that we encounter into images and impressions that are acceptable to, and understood by, our physical selves.

Everything in the universe is made up of, and manifested as, varying

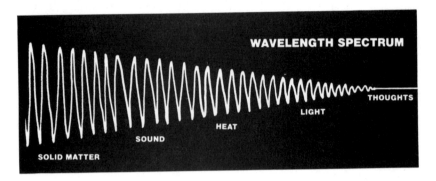

WAVELENGTH SPECTRUM

THOUGHTS

LIGHT

HEAT

SOUND

SOLID MATTER

rates of vibrations or wavelengths. At the bottom of the spectrum, with the slowest vibratory rate, is solid physical matter. The vibrations in the atoms that make up the molecules are not readily perceivable to us. Above physical matter, at a faster rate of vibration, is sound. Faster wavelengths than sound become the sensation of heat. Beyond heat is the impression of light. The observation could be extended to include thoughts, at a wavelength or vibratory rate faster than electricity or light.

Within each relative classification of sensations in the broad scale of vibratory rates, are manifestations varying with the speed of the waves. Within the classification we call light, for instance, are slower waves which appear red, and faster waves which appear blue. Within the classification we call sound, are slower waves that are heard as low rumbling tones and faster waves that are heard as high shrill pitches.

It is also interesting to note that the qualities of the vibratory manifestations and their resulting images are not fixed entities themselves, but are relative to the sensory receptor perceiving them. It is fairly accepted knowledge today that there are sounds that cannot be heard by humans and yet are definitely audible to certain animals. There are light impressions that are imperceptible to plants and animals and yet quite real for humans. Modern communications technology provides even more dramatic examples of altering the images of a fixed set of vibrations, by altering the sensing receptor. Visual images can be transformed into electronic impulses which can be further altered to become sounds, which can then prompt the generation of physical substance (a television camera scans the surface of Mars; the data is transmitted by radiowave to earth; a computer rearranges the data and produces a color print of what the camera "saw"). If it were easier to affect the sensory receptors of our physical bodies, perhaps we humans could simply will ourselves to hear colors, taste sounds, or feel odors for additional perspective in our daily lives or in times of special importance.

Though literal concepts of varying wavelengths and vibratory rates were unknown to the mystics of feudal Japan, their teachings nonetheless stressed the uniform structure and common source of all things. From this belief that all things are varying manifestations of the universal source (everything fits in somewhere on the vibratory rate scale), ninja developed the attitude that there are no totally independent actions or objects in the realm of existence. Seemingly unrelated phenomena can actually be linked together in interaction. As a result, a vast realm of subtle and yet direct control over our surroundings is available to all of us, if only we would acknowledge and accept that control.

The ninja of old used his mind to observe, visualize, and affect his surroundings by harmonizing the vibrations of his thoughts with the varying wavelengths of the environmental aspects he wished to alter. Beginning with simple exercises that teach the effectiveness of the method, the ninja was encouraged to develop the power of the mind to clarify his intention and work his will without actions.

As an initial step, students of ninjutsu are admonished to become actively aware of the ease with which the senses become dulled over the years. Stripping away the impediments and sharpening the senses is a crucial beginning to the task of learning to perceive and interact with outside forces in a pure and direct manner.

This type of awareness approaches that of the animals, whose active consciousness is of a different order than man's. The consciousness of an animal is strongly fixed in the present moment, and the animal is relatively unaware of a past or future in the way a human being is. The animal awareness is not hindered by memories or considerations of potential outcomes, and is exclusively locked into each existing instant as it occurs. Though the animal does not have the advantages of guidance from the past or direction for the future, it is free to pick up a whole range of subtle present environment impressions that are largely crowded out or ignored by humans. Sense impressions from infrared or ultraviolet light, cosmic rays, air pressure, or magnetic fields are as real for animals as traffic signals, printed words, and verbal expressions are for humans.

The first step toward personal control and the exercise of power in one's world is to merely be aware of one's body and the effects of its surroundings. A key point in the study of all aspects of ninjutsu is the development of total naturalness at any chosen level of awareness. The martial art training begins with basic physical movements and from there moves on to specialized combat skills. In relearning the naturalness of our fundamental physical nature, we are subtly forced to recognize the effects of cluttering ourselves up with unnecessary, unnatural actions in the past. Once we experience the impossible-to-avoid physical manifestations of unnatural conditioning, we can then move inward to the mind and emotions and see how we have stretched the inner-self out of shape as well.

The awareness-development exercises of ninjutsu training are complementary to the overall attitude of complete growth and realization that are inherent in the art. Various other martial arts, religions, or exercise and enlightenment systems insist that the practitioner give up his humanness in order to attain the desired goals. The senses and corporeality seem to be regarded as embarrassments or evil tricks of the universe, created for the sole purpose of being overcome or transcended. Wholesome food, sexuality, and emotional richness are deemed as limiting, and are to be sacrificed for enlightenment. In the more perverted systems, the human qualities are looked upon as sins to be washed from the personality and apologized for.

As a comprehensive lifestyle, the ninjutsu regards the body and its sensual capabilities as tools for the accomplishment of life's purposes. As such, they are to be acknowledged for their value, well-cared for, and fine-tuned. Any spiritual system that denies or represses the natural physical requirements and proclivities of the body will create a grave state of imbalance that must be dealt with eventually before any true spiritual advancement can be attained. The teachings of ninjutsu advocate the development of the total entity, with all its naturally-endowed balances and polarities, and they reject as senseless and needlessly brutal any system, martial or religious, that demands suffering, repression, self-debasement, or the abdication of joy in life for the sake of attaining transcendent consciousness or so-called salvation.

EXERCISE ONE—Earth Element

As you awaken at the beginning of the day, keep your eyes closed and allow yourself to acknowledge any fragrances or odors you notice. The smell might be overpowering like the aroma of coffee and bacon coming from the kitchen, or it might be a subtle scent like traces of mothballs in the blanket. You may not be aware of any smell at all. Allow yourself at least two minutes with your eyes closed to search round for all the variations that your nose can pick up. As you arise, affirm to yourself that you will be especially aware of your sense of smell today for the entire day.

It would be particularly effective if you could pick a day that would take you through many different environments in order to give you a wide range of stimuli. Allow yourself to notice all smells, pleasant or otherwise. Do not make value judgments about the day's odors, labeling things as good or bad. Simply be aware of the effects that the odors and fragrances have on you in all ways. You may be surprised that some odors conventionally labeled as "bad" may occasionally seem pleasant to you. Mentally assume that anything you smell today will have a pleasant odor. Close your eyes to experience subtle odors and see if particular emotions or memories come to mind. Do not limit yourself to obvious smells like flowers or automobile exhaust fumes on the road. Smell the television set as you sit and watch it, the pencil as you write with it, and the wallpaper as you walk down the hall. Notice the effects that the smells have on you.

Throughout the day, pause periodically to consciously take a deep breath. With your spine straight, breathe in through your nose and take the air deep into your lungs. Let your stomach push out as far as it can, and hold your lungs at total expansion for a few seconds before exhaling. When you breathe out, briskly push the air out through your nose until you have forced all the breath from your lungs.

EXERCISE TWO—Water Element

As you awaken in the morning, one or two days after carrying out exercise one, keep your eyes closed and allow yourself to acknowledge any tastes you notice. Run your tongue around your teeth and gums, open your mouth slightly and taste the air as you breathe in, or run the tip of your tongue along the knuckles of your fist. Allow yourself a minute or two with your eyes closed to experience whatever affects your sense of taste. As you arise, affirm to yourself that you will be especially aware of your sense of taste today for the entire day.

It is not necessary to adjust your diet for the day; in fact it is recommended that you eat the foods you would normally consume. The difference for the day is in the degree of attention you direct to your sense of taste. Eat all foods in a slow and deliberate manner. Close your eyes when you can, to enhance your awareness of the favors. Do not divert your attention through conversation or idle distractions, and take twice the normal time to chew each mouthful of food. Before you place something in your mouth, see if you can imagine or create the impression of the taste you will experience. Imagine that every bite contains a new taste sensation, no matter how familiar the food may really be. Mentally assume that anything you taste today will have a pleasant and exciting flavor.

EXERCISE THREE—Fire Element

As you awaken in the morning, one or two days after carrying out exercise two, open your eyes and allow your sight to take in whatever is directly in front of your eyes. Without moving your body at all, adjust your visual focus for a variety of distances. Look across the room at some object and its shadow. Blur your vision intentionally and see what automatically comes into focus. Shift your concentration from the blanket next to your face to something at medium range. Allow yourself at least two minutes to experiment with your sense of sight and the focusing mechanism of your eyes. As you arise, affirm to yourself that you will be especially aware of your vision today for the entire day.

Close your eyes and exert gentle pressure against your eyelids with your fingertips. Vary the angles and intensity of the pressure, and notice the changing colors and patterns that you see. As you observe the visual impressions, be aware of the fact that you are creating the sights you behold, and that their reality is a product of your own mind reacting to stimuli.

Throughout the day, be especially conscious of the effects of color intensity around you. Notice how colors are used to create specific impressions or subtle emotional responses. See which colors are the most attractive to you and which colors are predominant in your clothes closet. Occasionally blur your vision slightly so that color images take precedence over the utility value or meaning of things around you. As you behold the colors, see if any emotions or memories come to mind.

A second area of visual awareness should be "new" sights in familiar areas. Observe your normal viewing patterns to become aware of how much visual input you filter out. Close your eyes and see if you can remember the color and pattern of a co-worker's clothing for the day. Without looking out the window, try to remember how the day's weather appears. Look around familiar areas, pretending that you were blind until now.

Consciously look at the faces around you. Do not stare with an intensity that will make others uncomfortable; simply be there in their eyes. We often develop the habit of depersonalizing our contacts with fellow human beings by avoiding close visual attention. For the entire day devoted to this exercise, concentrate on being aware of looking into the eyes of others.

EXERCISE FOUR—Wind Element

As you awaken in the morning, one or two days after carrying out exercise three, keep your eyes closed and allow yourself to acknowledge the physical feelings you notice. Without moving at all, make a quick survey of your body, noting any impressions on your sense of touch. The feel of the cloth, the position of your limbs, heat or contact from a sleeping partner, should all be in your awareness. Allow yourself at least two minutes with your eyes closed to take in all the variations that your sense of bodily awareness can pick up. As you arise, affirm to yourself that you will be especially conscious of your sense of touch today for the entire day.

As you proceed through the day, consciously experience as many varying stimulations to your tactile sense as you can. You may be surprised that some feelings conventionally labeled as "bad" may occasionally seem pleasant to you. Mentally assume that anything you feel today will be a pleasant sensation. Be aware of cool and warm temperature variations around your body. Consciously take part in all muscular actions you perform, whether it involves running, chewing, or moving objects about. Notice the sensations produced by the clothing on your body. Observe your resistance to, or compliance with, the rocking motions of vehicles you ride in.

At one point during the day, find a quiet comfortable place in which you can lie down on your back. Relax your body, spread out, and allow the concerns of the day to leave your consciousness. Close your eyes and take a full breath of air. Imagine that you are breathing the air all the way to the bottom of your body cavity, and feel your lungs expand as much as they can. Repeat this deep breathing two or three times to clear your mind and lungs. Next, begin to tighten your body, starting with the very center at your solar plexus. Feel the tenseness move through your body trunk, simultaneously working up, down, and out to the sides while retaining the muscular tension in the center. Hold the tension as you move your consciousness out through your body, tensing every muscle as you go. At the final stages, curl your fingers and toes inward and exert complete tension in all the muscles of your body. At that point, you should virtually be bouncing off the surface on which you are reclining. Suddenly release the tension, relaxing all your muscles at the same time while letting go of your breath. Proceeding up one limb at a time, consciously relax each muscle until your body is totally limp, deadweight. Begin with the fingers and toes and move inward to the center of your body. Consciously feel each muscle as you let it go.

Throughout the entire tactile-sense day, be aware of any tension that you might unconsciously store in the muscles of your shoulders, face, stomach, or thighs. Acknowledge that you put the tension there for some purpose, and release it.

EXERCISE FIVE—Source Element

As you awaken in the morning, one or two days after carrying out exercise four, keep your eyes closed and allow yourself to acknowledge any sounds you notice. The noise might be overpowering like the sound of your ringing alarm clock, or it might be a subtle sound like the traffic moving by in the street outside. You may not be aware of any sounds at all. Allow yourself at least two minutes with your eyes closed to search around for all the tonal variations that your ears can pick up. As your arise, affirm to yourself that you will be especially aware of your sense of hearing today for the entire day.

Throughout the day, be conscious of the effects of the voice qualities displayed by people around you. See which tones, volume levels, and accents affect you in positive and negative ways. Be observant of the ways others' voices affect the people around you. Use a tape recorder to record your own voice as you read sections of this book out loud. Compare what you hear from the tape recorder with your mental concept of the sound of your own voice. If that were a stranger's voice, what would be your reaction to that person, based on the voice quality alone?

A second area of sound awareness should be your bodily reactions to musical notes. Allow yourself to be exposed to a variety of different types of music. Relax in a seated position with your eyes closed and your attention fully directed toward the music. Notice the reactions in different parts of your body when different musical types are experienced. Notice if there is no physical reaction at all. See if your mind automatically creates scenes or situations under the influence of the music. Follow the scenes out for awhile and then return your consciousness to the music itself.

At some point during the day, find a place where there is no sound at all. Relax there for several minutes and allow your hearing to grow accustomed to the silence. Become aware of the steady sound behind the silence, that takes the place of the constant noise that usually assaults the ears. Observe what that silence sounds like.

As a logical progression in learning to combine pure bodily awareness with the mental processes, the student of ninjutsu is taught to observe the action of the mind, in combination with regulation of the breath, to direct the body's energies in order to adapt his mood to a particular situation or set of circumstances. This selection of consciousness permits the ninja to fit-in appropriately with the situation at hand, or to change his perspective in order to affect the direction of the events that make up the situation.

EXERCISE SIX—Earth Level

When feeling overly excited, extremely nervous, or too emotionally involved, the ninja would practice a method of controlled breathing and mental imagery to calm and ground himself and bring his feelings back "down to earth."

Direct all your attention to your breathing. Allow yourself to inhale slowly, totally filling your lungs and pushing your abdomen all the way out. It should take you approximately eight seconds to take a full breath. Do not hold the breath with the lungs and abdomen fully extended, but immediately breathe out slowly until you have forced all the air from your lungs and pulled your abdominal muscles in to their normal, relaxed position. The exhalation should also take approximately eight seconds to complete.

As you carry out this particular breathing cycle, imagine that your entire body cavity is hollow, as though it were a huge empty cave. As you breathe in, feel the air rush in along the back of your throat and down along the back of the "cave." Take the air all the way in, as though it were going to the bottom of the body cavity. You should feel the inhalation pressure in your genitals and lower abdomen. Immediately exhale, forcing the air up and out along the front of the "cave." Inhalation and exhalation should be total, and one should turn into the other without pause.

It may be helpful to visualize a symbol of the earth element while you are performing this breathing exercise. Close your eyes and picture a range of mountain peaks in the wilderness. Narrow your vision to the highest of the peaks. Picture yourself seated on top of the peak, with one leg hanging over each side as though you were riding a camel. Imagine the feel of the mountain along the inside of your thighs and calves as though the mountain were gripping you, and allow your lower body to feel as though it were becoming a part of the mountain's roots and the very earth itself.

Use the visual image along with the specific breathing method to calm yourself and increase your feelings of stability in times of stress.

EXERCISE SEVEN—Water Level

When feeling unresponsive, too rigid, or enmeshed in the reasoning process, the ninja would practice a method of controlled breathing and mental imagery to increase his adaptability and flexibility, and to allow his feelings to "go with the flow."

Direct your attention to your breathing. Allow yourself to inhale slowly, totally filling your lungs and pushing your abdomen all the way out. It should take you approximately eight seconds to take a full breath. With the lungs and abdomen fully extended, hold the breath for approximately three seconds. You should feel the pressure of the breath pushing out against your abdomen, just below your navel. Breathe out by totally relaxing the lungs and muscles of the ribs while simultaneously reversing the pressure on your lower abdomen. The tightening of these muscles should force the air out of your lungs with a brisk rush. Maintain the inward abdominal pressure for three seconds before breathing in again.

It may be helpful to visualize a symbol of the water element while you are performing this breathing exercise. Close your eyes and picture a rocky coastline along the ocean. Narrow your vision to a small stretch of boulders, around which the waves are breaking. Picture yourself sitting in an inflated seat, up to your hips in the deep water. Imagine the feel of the wave currents as they shift you about from one direction to another. Mentally relax and become a part of the natural rhythm and flow.

Use the visual image along with the specific breathing method to become more sensitive and come closer to your inner feelings in times when emotional flexibility is needed.

EXERCISE EIGHT—Fire Level

When feeling low on energy, indecisive, or manipulated by others, the ninja would practice a method of controlled breathing and mental imagery to recharge himself, gain command of his own direction, and "fire up" for the activity at hand.

Direct all your attention to your breathing. Relax your lungs and the muscles of your ribs and take in a quick breath by pushing out on the abdominal muscles covering your stomach. The breath should come in with a rush, and you should feel the pressure behind your solar plexus. Do not hold the breath with your ribs expanded, but immediately breathe out briskly by inwardly tightening the muscles beneath the solar plexus. Maintain a relaxed feeling in your ribs and shoulders throughout the repetitive inhalation/exhalation cycles, and use the muscles below the tip of the sternum and above the stomach to move the air in and out of your body rapidly.

It may be helpful to visualize a symbol of the fire element while you are performing this breathing exercise. Close your eyes and picture an old-hearth stone fireplace in the center of the open area, and see the red hot coals used for heating iron to the point where it can be shaped and molded. Picture yourself in front of the coals, with your lungs taking the role of the wind bellows. Imagine the feel of the flames as they leap up with every exhalation, and the intense heat that radiates through your solar plexus with every inhalation.

Use the visual image along with the specific breathing method to generate psychic energy, and to increase your feelings of personal control of the situation in times when purposeful action is needed.

EXERCISE NINE—Wind Level

When feeling intellectually pressed, emotionally controlled, lacking in compassion or too self-oriented, the ninja would practice a method of controlled breathing and mental imagery to increase his feelings of being in touch with others and transcendent of his baser powers.

Direct your attention to your breathing. Relax your lungs and the muscles of your ribs, and take a quick breath by pushing out on the abdominal muscles covering the stomach. The breath should come in with a rush, pushing your stomach out and filling your lungs. Hold the breath for approximately three seconds, being aware of the pressure in the center of your chest. Slowly release the breath in a steady, controlled stream, by gently tightening the muscles around your ribs and pulling up and in on the muscles of your abdomen. You should feel a tightening in the center of your chest, and the exhalation should take approximately ten seconds to complete.

It may be helpful to visualize a symbol of the wind element while you are performing this breathing exercise. Close your eyes and picture a vast forest of tall trees. Narrow your vision to a portion of the forest along a high ridge exposed to the wind. Picture yourself standing among the trees, and feel the wind moving around you. Imagine the feel of the wind as it moves on, slipping around and by anything that gets in its way. Feel the wind that your breath creates as you share the air with everything around you.

Use the visual image along with the specific breathing method to increase your consciousness of your benevolent nature, and to strengthen your intellectual grasp of any situation.

Certain electromagnetic channels of the body are said to be the most sensitive in the feet and hands. Ninjutsu's *kuji-in* (nine mudra hand seals) and their variations make up an attitude-control system based on direction of energy through the hands. The thumb represents the ku source element, with each of the fingers representing one of the four elemental manifestations.

Water (sui)

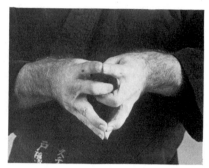

Fire (ka)

Earth (chi)

To encourage more of a chi (earth) stability and strength, the little finger is folded to form a ring with the thumb, which is interlocked with the little finger and thumb of the other hand.

Water (sui)

To encourage more of a sui (water) adaptability and power, the ring finger is folded to form a ring with the thumb, which is interlocked with the ring finger and thumb of the other hand.

Fire (ka)

To encourage more of a ka (fire) aggressiveness and energy, the middle finger is folded to form a ring with the thumb, which is interlocked with the middle finger and thumb of the other hand.

Wind (fu)

To encourage more of a fu (wind) sensitivity and harmonious action, the pointer finger is folded to form a ring with the thumb, which is interlocked with the pointer finger and thumb of the other hand.

Earth (chi)

Wind (fu)

It should be noted that the suggested visualizations that accompany the breathing methods in this chapter are by no means the only possible mental aids. The images have been presented as a guide or format for consideration. Some ninja would visualize different animals that represented the four qualities, such as the bear for the earth, or the dragon for the wind. Some would imagine the feeling of the body's life force flowing from one or two body centers to the deficient center. Others would find it more helpful to hold their concentration on a single word while affecting their breathing, such as "agility" or "flexibility" for the water element, or "intensity" or "drive" for the fire element. Any one of the visualizations is a mere trick, at any rate, for the purpose of locking the mind's activity onto the endeavor at hand—the adjustment of the body's metabolism and direction of the personality's approach to the everchanging demands of present-moment reality.

The physical breathing techniques themselves, on the other hand, represent a more concrete aspect of bodily control. By consciously regulating the organs that control the rates at which the air enters and leaves the bloodstream, and by applying pressure to those areas of the body in which the endocrine glands function, the body can be made to alter its pace and adapt to new situations as they arise.

Additional perspective can be given to the validity of the breathing methods by observing natural responsive breath patterns in different life situations. Notice the way your body adjusts the breathing rate and depth to naturally handle conditions of stress, emotion, concentration, or fatigue. External environmental factors, whether real or imagined, trigger specific psychophysical responses that stimulate or restrict the activity of the endocrine glands and cause the adjusted metabolic rate to alter the breathing cycle. As a result of this stepped procedure, the body is enabled to handle a wide range of daily encounters. By reversing the process, and adjusting the breathing rate and then mentally suggesting a specific quality of mind, the body responses associated with the breathing rate and state of mind can be artificially induced to allow the desired approach to the situation at hand.

It is a futile exercise to attempt to control one's surroundings without first learning to control one's own perceptions of and reactions to the surroundings. Power begins in the center of our beings, and awakening to that reality is a natural development of training in ninjutsu. ■

CHAPTER 5

**ACTIVE MEDITATION:
The mind-sharpening
methods of the ninja.**

The mind directs
  the energy of the physical entity
  into harmony with the state of the universe.
When all about you is frantic chaos,
  do not be absorbed by the crashing of gongs,
  the screams of the hysterical,
  or the wailing of the grievous.
Become one with the rocks that never feel the need
  to weep.
Become a part of the plains that never feel the need
  to shift about at the whim of minor happenings.
Your roots are buried deep.
Like those of the mountains.

For the student of ninjutsu, understanding the mind and its workings is crucial to development as a competent fighter. The brain is a valuable self-defense tool that is often overlooked in many martial arts training systems. Physical conditioning and technique memorization can take the practitioner only so far, and the advanced fighter must go on to develop the qualities of awareness and detachment.

This detachment is an ability to figuratively back-off from activity in which you are engaged and observe the total picture of you and your adversary. Instead of concentrating on what you are going to do, you simply observe the attacker's actions from a defensive pose and react appropriately to his moves. Instead of concentrating on beating your adversary, you allow him to make the mistakes that will bring about his downfall.

One aspect of effective self-protection or effective martial arts training is total involvement in the activity from moment to moment. The minute your attention or awareness begins to slide forward or backward from the present instant, you are no longer "there." Mentally verbalized thoughts such as "Here's what I'll do if . . ." or "Why did I let . . ." are hindering to present-moment, spontaneous response because the fighter is thinking of himself as isolated from the action, both physically and in terms of time frame.

Take a few minutes to recall your most frustrating moments in the training hall or in actual self-defense. Perhaps you were sparring with a training partner who was giving you a difficult time (and so you tried harder to beat him, filling the air with all your thoughts of what you should do or should have done, making it even easier for him to pick up your intentions and control you). Perhaps it was in an actual combat encounter (and your thoughts of the harm or injury he could possibly do to you hindered your natural skills and forced you to take a defensive attitude resulting in a tough time handling the situation). Perhaps you were learning a new and difficult technique (and you kept your mind on all that you were doing wrong, and you worked so hard at "trying" to do the technique that you actually felt you were getting worse at it instead of better).

Successful activity and exciting living depends on 100 percent involvement in whatever you are doing at any given moment. When the mind begins to wander, drifting to other times or conjuring up all sorts of pointless non-existent situations (worries and regrets), the quality of the body's activities decreases and the total potential of the moment is robbed. Become totally involved, however, and the very intensity of what you are doing and thinking will capture the moment entirely.

In terms of self-defense fighting, a student must first go through intensive physical training so that he will know what actions are appropriate for various attacks and attackers. In the physical level of training, the student must trust his teachers and accept what they teach him from their experience. This physical training period is a time for coming to know what works best for each personal body build. The actions of the muscles and bones, breath regulation, and the body's dynamic force are all aspects of this first major practice level.

Beyond fundamental physical training is the control of the mind's activity, which is more difficult than one might think. Physical weaknesses or shortcomings are easily observed by others, and they can be remedied by suggestions from an observing teacher. Darting eyes and fidgeting hands betray nervousness. Locked knees will prevent swift, balanced movement. Drawing a fist or shoulder back will warn the adversary that a punch is coming. However, only you can know what is going on in your mind. No one can reach in there to see what you are doing or help you.

Zen style meditation is a good way to practice this mental discipline and awareness. The Zen concept is very misunderstood in the West, however, and many erroneously believe meditation to be a means of "freaking out," fading from reality, or entering a dream world of artificial perceptions. The meditative state is actually a state of intensified awareness, not sluggish drowsiness. Meditation is used as a means to total effectiveness in physical endeavor.

EXERCISE ONE

Simple Meditation

Find a reasonably quiet place where you will not be disturbed. Do not seek total silence, as a few natural noises will actually help. If you wish, you can place a mat on the floor or ground for comfort, and you should have a small, firm pillow nearby. Sit in the middle of the mat with your legs outstretched. Draw the left foot toward you, and place the heel in the crotch with the sole resting against the right thigh. Insert the outer edge of the right foot between the calf and thigh of the left leg. Lean forward and pull the pillow in under your seat so that it is in a comfortable position. Raise and straighten your body trunk, with the back slightly arched so that the stomach and chest are pushed forward. Rest the right hand palm-up in the left hand, with the thumb tips touching. The hands should be tucked into the lap tightly, with the elbows close to the body trunk.

It should be noted that the traditional meditation pose has nothing inherently potent or magical about it. Sitting in a Western ladder-backed chair with the hips as far back as possible and the feet firmly planted on the ground can produce similarly satisfactory conditions for successful meditation. The Eastern meditation pose is recommended when possible, however, in that the supported back in a chair can permit too much bodily relaxation and lead to drowsiness and sleep. The traditional pose also provides the benefit of teaching consciousness of the proper healthful posture.

Stretch the spine to the ceiling and then settle it. Let the shoulders fall naturally. Rock back and forth and from side-to-side several times to get the feel of the vertical centerline. Look straight ahead and then lower your chin until the eyes come to rest on the floor about two meters in front of you. Pull the chin in as far as you can. Lower the eyelids to shade the eyes, but do not close the eyes. Close the mouth and breathe through the nose. This seated posture is the basic position for meditation practice. The folded legs help to keep tension on the lower spine which will keep the back straight. Remember to keep the chin tucked in and the back slightly arched.

From this seated posture, you can begin to learn how to observe from within. In essence, you are seeking your "self."

Feel yourself breathe. Allow yourself to concentrate totally on feeling the breathing action. Something can feel the breath going in and out, and the stomach rise and fall. Something is aware of the sound of your breathing.

Repeat the word "ninja" to yourself. Somewhere in your head, something can hear the word. Try to watch the something that can hear your thoughts.

Clench your hands into fists and then return them to the meditation position. Something watches the hands move. Something quite apart from the hands observes the action. Try to watch the observing something as it considers the hands.

We might at first think of this observer in ourselves as simply being our mind at work watching our bodies. But there is more complexity than that. For if we think the word "ninja" to ourselves, the observer can watch the mind itself at work.

What is this thing that watches everything as though it were apart from us? We will call it The Observer. It is a point of awareness that is really above consciousness, thinking of thoughts, and even the emotions. It is the thing that you probably refer to when you say "I." This Observer is your awareness, and when The Observer is not present, you are in a distracted state, or daydreaming as things go on around you.

Practice calling up this Observer and using it to look at things. If you are breathing, The Observer watches the breathing. If you are nervous, The Observer can watch the nervousness; that's how you know that you are nervous. Experiment with the observations so that you come to know and understand how The Observer works.

EXERCISE TWO

Training The Observer

Once you recognize The Observer in you, you may begin to train The Observer to do what you want it to do. In normal people, The Observer tends to run the consciousness. This results in scattered thoughts, lack of awareness, or mind wandering as The Observer skips around picking up anything that comes along. This freshness of The Observer is called "wonder" and is desirable and good. However, there are times when we need to control The Observer to prevent our emotions or outside happenings from taking us over.

This second exercise is known as "breath counting," and it is somewhat misleading in that it has very little to do with how to breathe. Counting breaths is a simple and straightforward means of using The Observer and limiting its scope to a particular duty.

Assume the seated posture described in the first exercise. Allow yourself to get settled and adjusted to your surroundings. Begin to concentrate your attention on your breathing. Take natural breaths, letting your stomach move in and out. Do not try to consciously control or regulate the breath. Just let it happen.

Begin to count the breaths with The Observer. Each time you breathe out increase the number by one. When you reach the number nine, begin again at one. Your body is taking care of itself, holding itself upright, breathing naturally, blinking and swallowing occasionally. Concentrate exclusively on The Observer's counting. Do not become upset if stray thoughts creep into the mind and you find The Observer involved with them. Simply be aware that The Observer has strayed and redirected the consciousness to the job of counting again. If you become too relaxed, the mind will be at rest with The Observer. You will find yourself counting "... fourteen, fifteen, sixteen. ..." Alert yourself, and pay attention again.

The exercise seems extremely easy at first reading. It is not, however. The simplicity is designed to make it easy to tell if you are doing the exercise effectively. It is not difficult to notice when the exercise is not being done properly. The object of this exercise is to be aware of what you are observing, and to not allow other things to interrupt the observation. This is harder work than it might seem.

Begin with short periods of observing meditation. It is less discouraging to begin with ten minutes of meditation and gradually increase with each sitting. By the end of the two weeks you should be meditating ("observing") for 20-minute periods.

Distractions will occur, of course. Noises, visual objects, or thoughts will suddenly grab your attention. Do not be upset with the distractions. Simply notice them and return to your concentration. Physical discomfort may get to you, also. If it interrupts your concentration, stay seated, "watch" the discomfort for a moment and then return to the counting. If you are concentrating on the mental activity exclusively, you are not likely to notice the minor discomforts at all.

Bear in mind that the results of this exercise will be applied to the ninja fighting method in later exercises. You are not counting for the sake of counting; rather you are counting for the sake of disciplining your concentration. To be successful at this breath-counting exercise, you must want to be successful. Keep doing it just as you did when you were learning to punch or shoot properly. If you are not mentally ready for this, the exercise will be more difficult than the most complex physical techniques.

EXERCISE THREE

Pure Observation

The first exercise dealt with proper body positioning and finding The Observer in your personality. The second exercise dealt with training The Observer to limit its scope and to concentrate its awareness. The exercise you should now begin trains The Observer to avoid verbalizing or mechanically structuring the observations.

Assume the meditation position. Hold some small natural object in your hand so that you can examine it. It is suggested that a man-made object not be used, as it might trigger memories or thoughts related to the use of the object.

Before beginning this exercise, it is a good idea to allow yourself to come to rest. Hold the object in your hands while sitting in the meditation position and temporarily forget it. Go back to exercise two and begin by observing your breath. If you feel confident in your ability to concentrate on counting, drop the one-through-nine routine and just observe the rising and falling of your abdomen as you breathe. Concentrate on this alone. After a few minutes, you should notice your breath becoming shallower and your mind becoming totally involved with what you are doing. Once this acclimation takes place, you may begin your object observation.

Examine the object (stick, rock, etc). with your eyes. Turn the object in your hands and really look at it. Observe your mind as you scan the object, and note your thoughts. You are probably verbalizing, or thinking actual words that describe the object, such as, ". . . flat, rough, flexible, dry . . ." The object of this training is to get your mind away from such verbalizing. Try to use your eyes as you would your sense of touch. Close your eyes and run your fingers over the object. You simply feel the object and are probably not using mental words to describe it to yourself.

Use your eyes again. Run your sight over the object as though you were feeling it with your eyes. Observe and take in all the features without thinking about words. You may be tempted to think words such as, ". . . it was cut off here . . ." or ". . . the sand rubs off in my hand . . ." but do not. Just as you notice a feature with your Observer, go on in your examination. Learn to cut off the distracting and time-consuming habit of mechanical thinking and simply observe without making value judgments.

Over a period of several weeks, use different objects in this exercise. Keep the point of the exercise in mind for the first few sessions. After a few sittings, the words describing the purpose should be forgotten, and you should be on your way to development.

EXERCISE FOUR

Unconscious Consciousness

The purpose of this exercise is to bring the total body into the meditation process without destroying or disturbing the meditative state.

We all have the ability to use our bodies in relaxed, unconscious movement and to do many things in everyday activity that utilize this ability. Usually, familiarity with a physical action brings about this unconscious ability. We enter a room at night, find that it is dark, and run our hand along the wall in an upward manner, flipping the lights on. We do this automatically without going through the conscious process of discovering the dark, wondering what to do about it, searching for a light switch, and deciding whether to flip it up or down, all in a deliberate manner. We might be conversing with friends while climbing out of a swimming pool. Someone throws us a towel, and we catch it and begin drying off without interrupting our speech. We do not stop in mid-sentence, turn and line up with the thrower, hold our arms out protectively, and hold our breath until the towel hits us. Our catch is a graceful and natural one, and we hardly give it any notice at all.

To practice this exercise, assume a natural standing pose. Lower your eyelids slightly to shade your eyes, and begin to narrow your concentration to your breathing. Allow yourself a few minutes to become accustomed to this relaxation. When you feel you have reached the settled state of meditative awareness, slowly slide back into a defensive posture with your weight on your rear leg and your body turned sideways toward your training partner. Maintain the shaded eyes and stomach breathing. Direct your attention to your training partner, and observe him with the same non-verbalized awareness that you practiced in exercise three. If he slides to the side, just watch him. Adjust your position if you must to keep him in sight. Do not be looking for anything or anticipating any moves. Simply watch him in a receiving manner as though you were a spectator at a performance of some sort. You should feel relaxed, yet aware.

From a distance of approximately two meters, your training partner attacks with a half-speed lunging punch at your face. Allow your body to move back and to the inside of his swing as you bring your leading arm up and outward to strike the inside of the attacker's wrist. In this exercise, the attacker should retreat after his single advance. As the interrupting fist moves away, you should return to the calmness of mind in the meditative state. Concentrate on your breathing if you need to quiet your mind.

After a few moments of settling in the defensive position, again observe your training partner in the non-verbalized manner that you developed before. Do not think about him, or about *not* thinking about him. Simply allow your eyes to take him in.

Your training partner next attacks with a front kick to your stomach or groin. Rock your weight back onto your rear leg and raise your front foot up, turning your toes inward. Allow the shin of his kicking leg to hit the sole of your extended foot. Keep your weight low over your rear leg so that you stop his kick without knocking yourself over.

The attacker should then retreat after his kick. As he moves away, you should return to the meditative state of awareness. Strive to keep your mind empty of emotions or considerations of your successfulness. Do not be concerned if your technique did not work exactly as you wished. Do not become excited if your technique stops his attack. Retain the feeling that you are an observer and that the completed exercise no longer exists. There is only the task of maintaining calm awareness in the present moment.

From the defensive position, observe the attacker as he winds up and throws a soft rubber ball at you. As the ball approaches you, leap to the side or duck to avoid it. Again, resume the defensive pose and frame of mind in preparation for his next attack. You should feel ready for anything that happens, and yet expect nothing.

Continue this practice method, utilizing any single-action strike, kick, or weapon attack and its counter. Individual creativity can be used once a basic familiarity with the process has developed. The purpose of the training is to learn how to observe and detect any attacking motion as it originates, and to successfully deal with it as it is carried out.

Meditation practice is beneficial in ways of gaining control of the mind's activity and control of the emotions. These improvements can be enjoyed by all. A major benefit to the ninja, or any martial artist, however, is the increased accuracy in fighting, made possible by the increased observation.

Remember that meditation training for the purpose of mind control can be more difficult than physical training at times. In effect, you are adjusting a part of your personality. Do not expect a dramatic or revolutionary change overnight. ∎

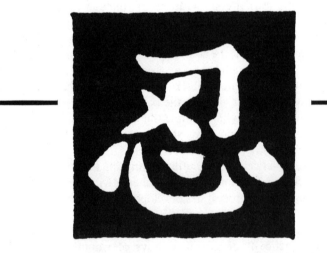

CHAPTER 6

EXTENDED REALITIES:
Knowing the unknowable,
perceiving the imperceptible.

You are not locked in that body of yours.
Your mind can soar and join other minds.
Do not be afraid
  to explore
  the dynamic potentiality of all things in the universe.
Quest ever on.
To know
  feel
  and be
  all that you possibly can.
Become a part of the ethereal
  and look down upon the earth as it plays its part in the cosmos.
Tap the knowledge of the heavens
  to see the scheme of impersonal totality
  and become a part
  of the mind and eyes of god.

What is that elusive quality beyond physical mastery of techniques that allows certain fighters the ability to prevail in all encounters? The household term is "sixth sense"—somehow knowing something that can't really be known. It is feeling that a puncher is faking a swing. It is an unconscious knowledge that something is wrong, just before an unarmed assailant pulls out a knife. It is knowing that an attacker awaits you in the parking lot with a pistol in his pocket. These and other skills of detection are developed by stripping away our faulty or clouded perceptions of things and events. We teach ourselves not to trust our impressions unless they are scientifically verifiable. All too often we ignore our subjective mental impressions or discount them as useless imagination, thereby robbing ourselves of a valuable source of input.

Beyond the five levels of physical consciousness, and the consciousness of the mind and its processes, lies a third realm of reality—an awareness of the unity and all-encompassing oneness that ties the universe together. This greater reality, or cosmic consciousness, is filtered through the mind and defined in ways that are understandable and acceptable to the physical organism.

According to the mystical heritage of the ninja, all individual things in the universe began as a single entity or "thought." From this universal beginning, all existence descended and divided into the limitless infinity of all things around us. It is crucial to recognize this concept in order to understand the basis of what we might call the spiritual capabilities of the original ninja. Though the grosser physical manifestations of all matter appear to be separate, there remains a subtle connection that links the essences of all in existence (i.e., electrons from a common source grouped to form atoms, which became molecules, which became physical objects). This is in direct opposition to theories that state that all things were created from the physical form upward, and are therefore unconnected (i.e., physical objects were created, and electrons and molecules were merely used to give the objects their structure).

Though there is a common tendency to classify things as being either physical or spiritual, there is actually no such dividing line. Acknowledging the body, its spiritual connection with all other things, and its mental interpreter, is not a statement of reality, but rather a reflection of our human way of looking at things. There is no such thing as spirit as opposed to physicalness, in that anything that we would call spiritual has physical reality as its base.

It may be true, however, that we are unable to understand how certain phenomena operate or come about, and until our physical science is capable of explaining it, we dismiss its mystery as being "of the spirit." Today, even the most down-to-earth and unimaginative individuals can wholeheartedly accept the concept of radio and television broadcasts as being totally within the range of physical reality. A few generations ago, however, the ability to send and receive words and images across miles of empty space would have been considered to be as other-worldly as ESP or transmutation of matter is today. Natural laws are constantly in operation around us. Our ability to use these laws to our own benefit depends on our sensitivity to their existence and our willingness to work with less than tangible phenomena.

Awareness of seemingly hidden natural factors can give the impression of supernatural powers. Strangers to the ocean find that sometimes it is easy to find the clams and sometimes the waves make it virtually impossible to come up with anything. The man equipped with a timetable for high and low tides, however, finds that it is always easy to get the clams. Those who know nothing of tide tables might see the knowledgeable one as a wizard who is able to command the elements, for whenever he goes to the sea, the waves are seen to fall back. Rather than learn the timetable themselves, they might find it easier to simply follow him whenever he went to the sea, or find it spiritually rewarding to place him in a position of reverence to which they could never hope to ascend. It would not be surprising if after his death, later generations would worship the man with the timetable as the divine one who could cause the clams to crawl from the sea onto his dinner plate by means of his will alone.

In a fashion similar to the preceding exaggerated story, the legends of the powers of the ninja came to be distorted and enhanced over centuries of Japanese culture. Imaginative tales were told of how the ninja had descended from the *tengu* (long-nosed winged demons who were half man and half crow). Popular stories often included ninja who possessed such skills as walking on water, disappearing through walls, transforming themselves into rats, or leaping and flying incredible distances. The true powers of the mystics of Iga, no matter how advanced they were in reality, paled when compared with the fantastic abilities of the glamorized ninja in the children's stories.

The historical ninja of feudal Japan were famous for their knowledge of the realm that we would call spiritual or occult today. Legitimate abilities practiced were the capability of detecting the threatening presence of others, reading the intentions of people, and visualizing distant places or persons. Advanced students of ninjutsu today still practice specific exercises for the development of the finer senses, and awareness of the seventh level of consciousness.

This seventh plateau of consciousness is an acknowledgment of the subtle effects we feel from the electromagnetic forcefield influences of others. Some students are more naturally predisposed toward developing the abilities, while others require longer training to make the exercises work for them. In either case, all persons will experience "off" days now and then. We do not question the possibility of basketballs going through net hoops just because we might occasionally miss a free throw. The mind exercises operate in the same manner. If we believe that the exercises are of any value to us, persistence is required.

EXERCISE ONE

Reaction Development

The first exercise is a method for developing a relaxed and open state of mind, and it reduces the tendency to anticipate the thoughts or actions of another. The practice method involves two or more training partners—a controller who will give the commands for action, and one or more receivers who will carry out the commands. The exercise is designed as a means of practicing correct "last-minute" responses to definite stimuli, instead of reacting too soon, or reacting and hesitating too soon, to the anticipated stimulus that is imagined to be on its way. On the physical level alone, the exercise is an effective means for beginning students to practice spontaneously the leaping and tumbling that are such crucial aspects of the ninja's combat system.

STEP ONE

Controller

Stand in the middle of an open area or large room in which there are as few physical obstructions as possible. Assume a comfortable, natural standing pose with the weight evenly distributed on both feet. Breathe with the abdomen in a natural manner.

Receivers

Take a position in a ring around the controller, along the outer periphery of the open-training area. Assume the hira no kamae receiving posture with the knees flexed and the arms outstretched. Breathe in a natural manner that will attune the body and mind with the wind (touch) level of consciousness.

STEP TWO

2

3

5

6

STEP TWO
Controller

Call out a two-word action command in a clear and unhurried voice with sufficient volume to be heard easily. The command should be chosen from the following possibilities:

Jump forward
Jump backward
Jump right
Jump left
Jump high
Jump low
Roll forward
Roll backward
Roll right
Roll left

To increase the complexity and challenge of the exercises for advanced students, occasionally reverse the word order of action and direction ("Right jump" in place of "Jump right") to take the total number of commands to 20.

Receivers

Maintain the centered hira pose while you listen for the command. Suspend your thinking process and simply take in the words of the controller. As soon as you have heard both words, immediately carry out the command. Each specific command should trigger the following precise response:

— Jump forward: Slam your hips forward, lifting your feet and keeping your shoulders over your hips.
— Jump backward: Slam your hips to the rear, lifting your feet and keeping your shoulders over your hips.
— Jump right: Slam your hips to the right, lifting your feet and keeping your shoulders over your hips.
— Jump left: Slam your hips to the left, lifting your feet and keeping your shoulders over your hips.
— Jump high: Spring upward, lifting your knees and feet as high as possible.
— Jump low: Drop to the ground, folding your body to as low a position as possible.
— Roll forward: Drop to a squatting position, fold your arms across your shins, and roll forward along your spine, ending up back on your feet again.

— Roll backward: Drop to a squatting position, pull your elbows in and your hands next to your cheek bones, and roll backward along your spine, ending up back on your feet again.

— Roll right: Drop to a squatting position, fold your right arm across your shins, and roll to your right along your arm, shoulder and back, ending up on your feet again.

— Roll left: Drop to a squatting position, fold your left arm across your shins, and roll to your left along your arm, shoulder and back, ending up back on your feet again.

STEP THREE
Receivers

Rise from the ground and assume the hira no kamae once again. Forget the preceding action and prepare to receive the next command.

The controller should continue to give the two-word commands, varying the interval between commands so that the receivers do not become set in any rhythmic timing pattern.

It should be stressed that this is not a competitive exercise in which the controller tries to fool or trick the receivers. The controller is there to aid in the development of the receiver, and should maintain a mental attitude of indifference, trying not to make the exercise any easier or any more difficult than it normally would be.

The exercise is an important one, in that it allows us to become familiar with the feeling of reacting unhesitatingly to our first impressions. The exercise should be experienced several times before moving on to the next exercises in this chapter.

EXERCISE TWO

Feeling Presence I

The second exercise is a beginning step for developing skill in detecting the presence of others. The practice method involves two training partners—a receiver who will experience the feeling of presence, and a controller who will determine at what point the presence is felt. Due to the electromagnetic characteristics of the human body, it might be helpful to practice the exercise with a training partner of the opposite sex, for the first few sessions.

STEP ONE

Receiver

Stand in the middle of an open area or large room in which there are as few sensual distractions (noise, smells, breezes, etc.) as possible. Assume a comfortable, natural standing pose with the weight evenly distributed on both feet. Allow your hands to hang loosely at your sides, and let your shoulders relax into their normal position. Take your time, shake your body out if you need to, and become totally relaxed.

Begin a process of slow deep breathing, concentrating on the exhalation and using your stomach to move the air in and out of your lungs. After two or three breaths, allow your eyes to close slowly as you continue your breathing rhythm.

Begin to imagine that your body is surrounded by its own radar-like forcefield, extending out from the skin surface in all directions much like your natural body heat radiates out from your skin. With your eyes closed, allow yourself to become more sensitive to this imaginary extension of your sense of touch. See how far out you think it reaches, and mentally picture the boundaries of this invisible power shell that encases you.

STEP TWO

Controller

Slowly and quietly position yourself in front of the receiver while he or she is concentrating on the closed-eye breathing and forcefield visualization. You should be approximately one meter away from the receiver. Allow a few seconds to pass and then slowly raise your right arm to a position pointing between his eyes. Your arm should be straight from the shoulder to the tips of your extended fingers, and your fingertips should end up about one hand-length distance from the receiver's face.

Hold your right hand palm-down with the fingers and thumb straight and pressed together. Slowly lean toward the receiver, moving your fingertips forward mere fractions of inches per second. As you approach the receiver's face, imagine that your arm and fingers are like a garden hose carrying a stream of water from the center of your body to a distant target.

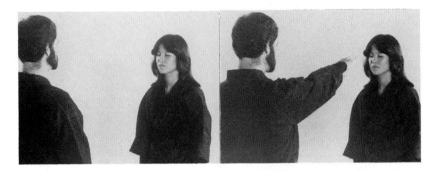

Imagine that you can feel and see the invisible-energy current as it flows through your spine, shoulder and arm, and out through the tips of your fingers. Allow your vision to focus on the receiver's brow, just above the nose and between the eyes. See the imaginary force as a beam of light that you are aiming at your training partner's face.

STEP THREE

Receiver

When you feel the presence of the controller's fingertips, lift your left hand to a palm-forward position just in front of your left shoulder. Maintain your relaxed standing position and keep your eyes closed as you raise your hand as a signal.

Controller

As you see the receiver's hand move into your field of vision, immediately freeze your action and maintain the distance between your fingers and the receiver's face.

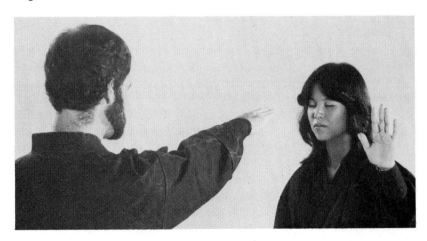

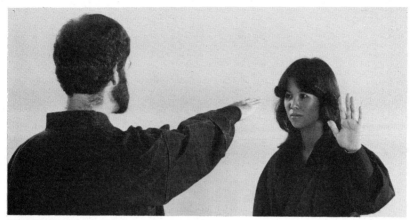

STEP FOUR
Receiver

Slowly open your eyes and check the position of the controller's hand.

All four steps of the exercise should be carried out with a leisurely pace, avoiding a sense of urgency. The controller should vary the time intervals between the beginning of the exercise and the point at which he or she aims the fingertips, so as to avoid setting up a predictable cycle.

If the receiver should continue to be unable to detect the controller's fingertips, all four steps of the exercise should be carried out slowly with the receiver's eyes only partially closed. In this way, the receiver can get a better feel for the experience being sought.

After several repetitions of the exercise, the controller and receiver should switch roles.

It should be stressed that this is in no way a competitive clash between the two training partners. It is a developmental exercise in which both students take turns assisting each other in discovering their own capabilities. The controller never tries to confuse or sneak up on the receiver. The controller is constantly concentrating his or her attention on properly carrying out the exercise so that the student assuming the role of the receiver can develop skill and confidence. At the same time, the receiver is not at all concerned with winning anything or impressing the controller. The receiver role is constantly concentrating his or her attention on properly carrying out the exercise, in order to learn to recognize and differentiate between actual stimuli and imagination. The purpose of the exercise is to actually *feel* the presence, and not merely guess correctly that the hand is there.

EXERCISE THREE

Feeling Presence II

This exercise is a slightly more advanced step for developing skill in detecting the presence of others. The practice method involves three or more training partners—a receiver who will experience the feeling of presence, and two or more controllers who will determine at what point and from which direction the presence will be felt. The third exercise is more difficult to carry out successfully than the second, due to the increased number of factors influencing the receiver. It is therefore highly important to avoid becoming entangled in "figuring out" the exercise, and attempting to explain it with rational concepts. Receiver and controllers alike should simply relax and have fun with the exercise, and not take it overly seriously.

STEP ONE
Receiver

Stand in the middle of an open area or large room in which there are as few sensual distractions as possible. Assume the shizen no kamae with the weight evenly distributed on both feet.

Just as in exercise two, begin a process of slow, deep breathing, concentrating on the exhalation and using your stomach to move the air in and out of your lungs. After two or three breaths, allow your eyes to close slowly as you continue your breathing rhythm.

As in the preceding exercise, begin to imagine that your body is surrounded by its own radar-like forcefield, extending out from the skin surface in all directions. With your eyes closed, allow yourself to become more sensitive to this imaginary extension of your sense of touch. Without moving, feel all around yourself, and imagine the sensation of something breaching your power-shell boundary.

STEP TWO
Controllers

Slowly and quietly position yourselves in a circle around the receiver while he or she is concentrating on the closed-eye breathing and forcefield visualization. You should all be approximately one meter away from the receiver and equally distant from each other. Allow a few seconds to pass and then use subtle facial or bodily gestures to determine which of the controllers will attempt to influence the receiver. When selected as the active controller, slowly raise your right arm to a position pointing at an imaginary band encircling the receiver's head at eye level.

Hold your right hand palm-down with the fingers and thumb straight and pressed together. Slowly lean toward the receiver, moving your fingertips forward mere fractions of inches per second. As in exercise two, imagine that your arm and fingertips are a hose transporting an invisible current of energy to the point at which you are aiming.

STEP THREE
Receiver

When you feel the presence of the controller's fingertips, lift your left hand into position in front of your chest. Use your thumb or first finger to

point in the direction from which you perceive the presence of the controller's fingertips. Maintain your relaxed standing position and keep your eyes closed as you raise your hand and point as a signal to the controllers.

Controller

As you see the receiver's left hand move up into pointing position, immediately freeze your action and maintain the distance between your fingers and the receiver's head.

STEP FOUR

Receiver

Slowly open your eyes and check the position of the active controller's hand.

As in exercise two, all four steps of this exercise should be performed at a leisurely pace, avoiding any undue haste or feeling that things should be speeded up. The controllers should vary their timing and selection sequence, in order to prevent setting up a predictable cycle. Just like the previous exercise, there is no sense of competition on the part of the controllers or receiver. The mind must be kept relaxed and open, and no sense of threat or pressures should interfere with these first steps toward confidence.

EXERCISE FOUR

Feeling Intentions

The fourth exercise is a beginning step for developing skill in detecting the intentions of others. The practice method involves two training partners—a receiver who will experience the feeling of the other's intention, and a controller who will determine from which direction or which side of the body the intention is felt. Exercise four is an important elementary technique for building up familiarity with subtle sensations of non-verbal communication.

STEP ONE

Receiver

Once again assume a relaxed, natural stance in the middle of an open area or large room in which there are as few distractions as possible. Allow your hands to hang loosely at your sides, and let your shoulders relax into their normal position. Take your time and become totally relaxed, breathing naturally by moving the air lightly in and out of the upper portions of your lungs.

Controller

Position yourself directly in front of the receiver, approximately one meter away. Raise both hands to a position next to your ears, above and slightly outside the boundaries of your shoulders. In this position your head and upheld arms should resemble the letter *W,* when you are viewed from the front. Allow your hands to be open and palm-forward with the fingers slightly curled inward, which is their normal relaxed state. Your eyes are aimed forward, focusing on the receiver's collar area at the base of his or her neck. There should be absolutely no tension in your arms or shoulders.

STEP TWO
Receiver

Allow your vision to rest on the controller's face. Do not stare into his or her eyes or concentrate at all. Relax and observe with a soft focus that takes in the whole picture.

Controller

Without making any physical movements at all, mentally choose one side of your body with which you will step forward and seize the receiver's collar or jacket lapel. While standing perfectly still, mentally visualize yourself stepping out and grabbing the receiver with the hand you have selected. Take your time and create a strong mental impression of your intention. Imagine that you can feel an invisible energy current as it flows through the spine, shoulder and hip, and arm and leg of the side you will move forward. Do all this in your mind and nervous system, and make no moves at all with your bones and muscles.

STEP THREE
Receiver

Maintain your soft visual focus and allow the subconscious or subjective levels of your mind to pick up an impression of the controller's intentions. You may pick up a strong feeling, or it may be nothing more than a subtle hunch, as to which side he or she will move. It may take only a split-second for you to know which hand and foot will come at you. You will move the opposite side of your body away from the side the controller advances.

Controller

Physically carry out your visualized intention by stepping forward and grabbing the receiver's collar or lapel with the side you have chosen (right foot and hand to the receiver's left lapel; left foot and hand to the right lapel). Move with about the same speed you would use when stepping forward and gripping a door handle. Do not fly out at the receiver in surprise, and do not creep out in slow motion. Continue the mental strength of your intention while you carry out the physical moves.

STEP FOUR

Receiver

As the controller moves forward toward you, step back and to the inside of his or her grasp, pulling your body out of reach. Move your hips first and keep your body in an upright posture as you assume the ichimonji defensive pose. Do not lean back or try to wriggle away from the grab. If the controller comes forward with the right foot and hand, you step back and to your right with your right foot. You may also need to drag your left foot back slightly to clear the controller's reach. If he or she advances with the left side, you slip back and to your left with your left side.

Do not race or jerk your body back. Your backward step should time out perfectly with the controller's forward step, to keep you at a safe distance if you were successful in picking up the intentions as he or she moved.

After each performance of the exercise, the receiver and controller should exchange roles, allowing a few seconds between each exercise in which to settle the mind and focus the consciousness. The time intervals between the beginning of the exercise and the point at which the controller physically moves should be varied, as should the right and left side, so as to avoid setting up a predictable cycle.

As with the other exercises in this section, it should be stressed that this is not to be treated as a competitive clash between the two training partners. It is a developmental training method in which both students assist each other in strengthening their own capabilities. The controller is always concentrating his or her attention on properly directing the feelings of the intentions. At the same time, the receiver is concentrating his or her attention on properly carrying out the exercise, in order to learn to recognize and respond to actual stimuli from others. The purpose of the exercise is to actually pick up the intention, and not merely to guess correctly which side will advance.

EXERCISE FIVE

Thought Projection I

The fifth exercise is a means of developing skill in projecting thoughts to others, and picking up the thoughts of others. The practice method requires a set of 25 easily prepared symbol cards, and involves two or more training partners—a receiver who will detect the thoughts, and one or more controllers who will project the thoughts. The fifth exercise is easy to carry out, and it does not involve any overt physical activity. Like the other exercises in this chapter, this procedure should be enjoyed and carried out with a relaxed attitude, and not worked at or analyzed. Have fun with it, and do not take it overseriously.

The symbol cards can be drawn on one sheet of paper from the patterns, and then duplicated on an office copier to obtain five sheets. The paper can then be glued on cardboard stock and cut into card shape, giving you five swords, five throwing stars, five fighting canes, five climbing ropes and five sickles, for a total of 25 symbol cards. The cards should show the picture symbol only, and should have no written words or other symbols on the face.

STEP ONE *Receiver*

Sit on the ground or in a chair in the middle of an open area or comfortable room in which there are as few sensual distractions as possible. You should have a pad of plain paper and a pencil or pen in front of you. Relax into a comfortable sitting position and be aware of the breath passing in and out through your nose, concentrating your attention in the upper portions of your nasal passages.

Controllers

Sit on the ground or in chairs behind the receiver, at least two arm-lengths away. You should have the shuffled deck of 25 symbol cards face-down in front of you, containing five copies of each of the five symbols. Position yourselves so that all controllers can see the symbol cards, and relax into a comfortable seated pose that will not distract your attention.

STEP TWO *Controllers*

Pick up the first card on the deck and place it back on the deck face-up. Concentrate your gaze on the exposed card, limiting your consciousness to the visual sense alone. See the design and "feel" it with your eyes. Do not mentally verbalize a word for the object pictured.

Quietly say the word "card," just loud enough to be heard by the receiver, and continue to concentrate totally on the symbol.

STEP THREE *Receiver*

Relax and allow your eyes to close lightly. With your eyelids lowered, look upward, as though viewing an imaginary black screen between your eyes. Allow the image of one of the five symbols to materialize on the black screen. The effect may take several seconds to produce or may appear instantly, and the symbol itself may appear clearly or may be nothing more than a hunch or abstract impression. There is no single proper method valid for all persons. Each individual will develop his or her own special way of recognizing the subtle impression as it is received. Once you have an impression, sketch it on the paper in front of you and number it with the figure 1. Increase this number by one with each subsequent round of the exercise.

Quietly say the word "next," just loud enough to be heard by the controllers, and redirect your concentration to the feel of the breath through your upper nasal passages.

STEP FOUR *Controllers*

Take the card from the top of the deck and place it face-up in the bottom position of the deck, and forget about it. Pick up the new top card and place it back on the deck face-up. Concentrate your attention on the exposed card, and continue through steps two, three and four repeatedly until you have gone through all 25 cards with the receiver recording his or her impressions for each card exposed. The original card will appear face-up in the deck to indicate that the full cycle has been completed.

To score the exercise, the controllers and receiver go through the deck together, comparing each card as it appears with its sequential position in the numbered list of drawings made by the receiver. Five correct matches out of 25, or 20 percent, reflects the natural one-out-of-five odds in the system. Any number of correct matches beyond five could indicate actual skill at picking up the thought impressions of others. Multiply the number of correct impressions by four to determine the percentage, and keep a continuous record of results for each person.

EXERCISE SIX

Thought Projection II

The sixth exercise is a somewhat more advanced training experience for the purpose of developing skill in projecting thoughts to others and in picking up the thoughts of others. The exercise involves two or more training participants—a receiver who will detect and carry out mentally visualized instructions, and one or more controllers who will devise and project mental commands for action. Though the sixth exercise can be carried out with a single receiver and controller, it is usually more effective and easier to produce successful results if one receiver works with a large group of controllers simultaneously visualizing the same instruction.

STEP ONE

Receiver

In a quiet room or corridor apart from the controllers, stand in a relaxed shizen no kamae natural posture, or move about with slow, undeliberate, natural movements. Keep your mind unfocused and quieted. Without concentrating or forcefully searching for thoughts, allow your consciousness to pick up any impressions that seem to appear in your mind.

Controllers

In a quiet room in which there are many small movable objects, such as a normal home living room with a television, stereo, wall-hung pictures, and random articles on tables or shelves. Select among yourselves an object and a simple action involving that object. It might be opening a window, turning off a light, or stacking certain books. Once you have agreed upon a common set of instructions, silently visualize the receiver carrying out the action. With your eyes shaded to reduce the possibility of distraction, imagine that you are watching the receiver stepping through each detail of the imagined command. Do not use words or verbalized thoughts; simply "see" the receiver carrying out the action.

After sufficient time for the group to agree upon and visualize a command in detail at least three times, a previously appointed controller should step out of the room to notify the waiting receiver that the exercise has begun.

STEP TWO

Receiver

Enter the room and follow any hunches or mental impressions that have appeared in your consciousness. Move to the area of the room in which you feel the controllers' instructions take you.

Controllers

Without verbalizing, continue to replay in your mind the scene of the receiver acting out your imagined instructions.

STEP THREE

Controllers

Use the sound of hand-clapping to assist the receiver in carrying out your wishes. As the receiver nears that section of the room in which the target object lies, use light hand-clapping to indicate that he or she is following your thoughts. Use loud hand-clapping when the receiver has touched the target object and loud, rapid clapping when he or she seems to discover and carry out the explicit action instructions. Stop clapping if the receiver leaves the target area or performs an action other than the target response.

Receiver

Continue to move about the room approaching objects under the guidance of your feelings and the controllers' applause.

STEP FOUR

Controllers

Verbally inform the receiver that the exercise has been completed once he or she has carried out the specific intended action. ∎

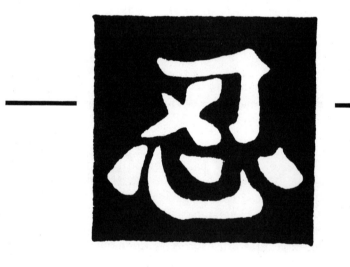

CHAPTER 7

THE ART OF UNDERSTANDING:
Seeing others through a
knowledge of the self.

The ninja gains his perspective
  by expanding his perceptions
  to see that everything is change
  and reality is temporary.
Approaching falsehood
  as though it were truth
  and truth
  as though it were falsehood
  the ninja finds no surprises.
There are times when strength
  is really a weakness
  laughter is power
  in *is* yo
  and innocence is wisdom.

O ne of the highest goals in ninjutsu training is the cultivation of the ability to move through all moments of living guided by personal, natural "knowing." Seeing through the clouds of deception in life situations, whether imposed by self or others, is a matter of clarifying our perception by removing the cultural and emotional barriers that we have permitted to grow up as blinders around us.

A working familiarity with the concept of *in* and *yo* balancing, referred to in Chapter One, is one direction from which we can approach the elimination of our limiting blinders. More commonly referred to as *yin* and *yang* in the popular media, this system of perception has encountered a widespread acceptance in recent decades. Unfortunately, like so many other abstract concepts that have been imported from the East and subsequently Westernized, the *in-yo* understanding has undergone substantial adjustments to allow it to fit with conventional Western beliefs. The system somehow seems to have been simplified and abridged to the point where it is a convenient analogy for explaining the supposed absolute opposites in the universe, the progression of all things and situations into something different, and the inevitability of good and bad reversing themselves. As handed down intact by generations of ninja, however, the concept has far more significance than a mere exotic label for the phenomenon of relativity.

It is taught that in the beginning, or actually before the beginning, there existed only a vast potential as a single thought or germinating cause. This concept is accepted by wide ranging belief systems, from Hinduism to "the way" of sage Lao Tzu's Taoism, to "The Word" of God in Christianity and Judaism. Though we can attempt to imagine what this original, total, all-inclusive existence was like, it is virtually impossible in reality for humans in our present state of evolution to conceive of such limitless vastness. We cannot overcome the fact that we are observers outside of, and looking at, the concept of the all-inclusive totality.

From this first stage of single totality, or *tai kyoku,* emerged the existence of fundamental polarities. Lao Tzu writes of the oneness of the tao becoming the duality of yin and yang (*in* and *yo* in the Japanese language), and the Bible states that God created the heavens and the earth, or the first polarity. Regardless of the symbols used to describe the phenomena, this polarity is nothing solid or concrete, but rather the potential individualization of all things in the universe. In essence, this fundamental polarity is the sexual concept of male and female on a cosmic scale.

In is the darkness, femaleness, the quality of "going to," or negative polarity. In this sense, the word negative does not have a disparaging or condemning meaning; it is used to indicate that which draws, attracts, and stores, as in a negative electrical charge or (−) magnetic pole.

Yo is the light, maleness, the quality of "going from," or positive polarity. These two qualities are said to have existed originally as potentialities alone. They became the fundamental separation of the oneness of the universe, which then permitted the further progression of pure energy into matter. The one became the two, and the two then became the essence of electrical energy charges, which eventually permitted the formation of electrons and subsequent atomic structure.

In past generations, ninja warriors developed a working knowledge of the *in-yo* concept as a strategy for bringing about desired results. Since all things emanated from a common universal source and developed into countless infinite possible relationships with each other, it is a matter of carefully repositioning our awareness in order to create alternate arrangements of the elements in any situation. The elements continue to exist, and their relationship is merely adjusted. The ways of *ten-chi-jin* of ninjutsu provide three different methods of approaching this altering process.

The principles of heaven, or *ten,* provide the means for the ninja to alter his relationship with his environment by causing his surroundings to change. The *in* and *yo* balance is shifted so that the ninja remains the same and the elements of the surrounding situation must change. By causing a more *yo* condition in his surroundings, the ninja increases the vulnerability of his enemy. The ninja makes his adversary want to fight even though he is unprepared. He causes the enemy to move when actually he wants to rest, and he causes the enemy to abandon advantageous positions. By causing a more *in* condition in his surroundings, the ninja decreases the threatening nature of his enemy. The ninja makes his adversaries wait when they are anxious to fight. He causes them to lose confidence in their knowledge and crowds them into narrow rooms or passages where they cannot take advantage of their superior numbers.

Combining an awareness of the five levels of personality as revealed in the elemental manifestations with the conscious control of the thought processes, and the intuitive reception, and acknowledgement of subtle vibrations from the surroundings, the historical ninja developed the skill of directing the personality and thoughts of others. This knowledge is one of the factual bases for the ninja's legendary ability to work his will without actions and achieve his goals without effort.

In broad terms, the direction of another's consciousness can employ either a positive or negative application, depending upon the purpose at hand and the receptiveness of the individual to be influenced. Some adversaries will consistently exhibit a particular style of behavior and epitomize one of the five elemental manifestations of personality. Others may fluctuate between personality traits as they are influenced by their environment, but they do have certain characteristic modes of behavior in which they are said to be "in their element." Through extensive self-evaluation exercises, the ninja builds the heightened intuitive sensitivity necessary for reading the lifestyle and personality of the target to be swayed. The successful utilization of ninjutsu's interaction with the five character styles is a product of the ninja's ability to know his adversary's most appropriate strength or weakness, to which a corrupting influence may be applied.

In psychological confrontations, using the earth influence, the adversary's resistance and fighting spirit are weakened by supplying him with enjoyable diversions. Under the water influence, the enemy's anger is prompted to lead him into vulnerability through rash and unthinking behavior. From the fire level of influence, the ninja creates fear and hesitancy in his enemy. Under the wind influence, the adversary is weakened by appealing to his sentimentality or soft-heartedness. Under the influence of the "emptiness," the ambitious or vain adversary is deceived by flattery and false loyalty.

This system of influences which manipulates an adversary's thought patterns is recognized as being a mere temporary interference in the playing out of long-range objectives. Whether influencing another individual for the sake of defeating him or for the positive purpose of gaining his cooperation, the results of the behavior alteration are, at best, temporary. Just as a boxer's feint loses its shock value after too many applications, the effectiveness of the personality tricks can wear off if an adversary becomes desensitized to their impact. Even positive manipulation of another's personality will take its toll on the ninja's mental qualities if they are carried out too long. Unceasing flattery of another's distended ego, or the continued soothing of the volatile temper of an irrational individual, will begin to affect the energy balance of even the strongest of determined ninja.

The principles of earth, or *chi,* provide an alternate way for the ninja to alter his relationship with his environment. The *in* and *yo* balance is shifted so that the ninja changes, and the elements of the surrounding situation remain the same. By assuming a more *yo* role, the ninja creates a favorable environment by increasing his leverage in a situation. When confronted by a powerful enemy, the ninja increases his own power to a level that surpasses his enemy's. When the adversary knows more, the ninja increases his knowledge in order to compensate. When outnumbered, the ninja increases his numbers. By assuming a more *in* role, the ninja creates a favorable environment by decreasing his vulnerability in a situation. When pursued by a furious enemy, the ninja drops back to a position behind his enemy. When his secret identity is uncovered, the ninja makes himself valuable to the enemy. When caught in a flood, he swims with the current.

Instead of directly affecting the personality or behavior of his enemy, the ninja can alter his own approach to any given situation. By expanding his perception in order to become aware of all the possible behavior and reaction mode choices that exist, the ninja can open up new insights into alternate outcomes for the situation being faced. In this manner, ninjutsu's chi grounding process provides a method for predicting the most likely future thoughts and actions of an adversary. By blending a working knowledge of the five personality styles, observation and recollection of personal reaction patterns, and intuitive sensing of unique case probabilities, the ninja can develop a predictable scheme of events, and then fit the likely occurrences with his own plans of action as appropriate for the desired results.

Inherent in this method of dealing with survival is the need to examine objectively the situation comprised by us and our adversary. We must avoid reading any values into his or our respective positions; instead we must observe our tactical relationship. When self-preservation is involved, there is a tendency to allow fear to assign non-existent advantages to the enemy facing us.

If your adversary awaits us in a darkened house, we may see him as having the advantage of being able to watch us without being observed, and thereby able to set up his attack. He seems to be in a fortress and we feel exposed. If an attacker confronts us with a knife, we may panic at the recognition of the fact that his weapon is an overwhelming advantage. If we are unfamiliar with knife fighting techniques, we may unthinkingly resign ourselves to being helpless. If we face an assailant who is huge in size, we may be totally intimidated by our comparative smallness. We may figure that one punch is all it would take to put us away.

Shifting viewpoints, however, can bring a completely altered perspective. By imagining ourselves to be in the place of our adversary, and then looking at all the weaknesses presented by the new outlook, we can use the tendency to see the negative to our own advantage. To see the other man's vulnerability, we put ourselves in his place.

As the killer concealed in the darkened house, we realize that we are trapped in there, and that tricks could force us out of our hiding place, or that we could simply be outwaited. As the knife fighter, we realize that our weapon causes our opponent to be extra-alert, that it gives him moral license to go to any extreme to defend himself. There is also a tendency to concentrate all the attention on the weapon, and forget the vulnerability or practical use of the other arm and legs. As the larger fighter, we realize how easy it is for a smaller opponent to move quickly and get inside our guard. We can also see how a small man can use his lower center of gravity to unbalance or throw us.

The principles of mankind, or *jin,* provide the means for the ninja to leave the situation exactly as it is, and create the impression of alternate realities through the use of illusion and the limited vision of others. The *in* and *yo* balance is stretched into exaggerated proportions so that the true relativity of the elements is obscured beyond recognition.

The major factor separating the methods of ninjutsu from ordinary fistfighting, everyday psychology, or conventional military action, is the application of *kyojitsu ten kan ho,* or deception strategy. Literally translated as "the method of presenting falsehood as truth," this strategy is applied to all of the ninja's activities. This reliance on misrepresenting the balancing elements of *in* and *yo* makes use of the psychology of preparing an adversary to think in one manner and then approaching him in another.

The tactic can be applied from varying extremes to confuse the adversary's perception of reality. Falsehood can be presented as truth. We can create the impression of strength in areas where we are, in reality, weak; or we can create the image of weakness to conceal our strengths. In the opposite sense, reality can be presented in such a way as to create the impression of falsehood. We can exaggerate our weaknesses to the point that adversaries feel they are being deceived, and then they hesitate to take action against us. We can also boldly present our strengths so that our enemies think we are bluffing, so they charge into our superior capabilities without sufficient strength or preparation.

Simple examples of the deception strategy as applied in the jin logical approach can be seen in unarmed fighting. Watch yourself in a mirror to see how your body looks as you prepare for and deliver a high punch. When working with a training partner later, drop your shoulder at the moment it becomes obvious that you are punching high, and punch to your opponent's ribs or stomach. The punch is not initiated, stopped, and restarted at a lower level. It is merely a low punch thrown with the body dynamics usually associated with a high punch.

In a closed-in clash where fists have turned into grappling hands, grab and pull your adversary toward you. He will probably instinctively try to pull away. As you feel his pull, change your motion to a push while stepping behind his foot and throwing him to the ground.

As you initiate an attacking counter defense, wind up and start a punch at your adversary's face. When he brings his forearm up to block, open your fist and apply a bone-breaking open-hand strike to the target his forearm presents.

Examples of the confusion tactics can also be seen in blade fighting. As you slash at your attacker's head with a sword or long knife, and as he attempts to block with a blade or metal bar, pull in suddenly with your arms, shortening your reach, and let the tip of your blade catch his forearm or hand.

A blade or stabbing weapon could also be concealed behind the arm by gripping the handle in an underhand manner with the blade extending up behind the back of the elbow.

In an actual self-defense confrontation against a blade-wielding assailant, you can assume a fighting position which suggests you are unskilled at self-protection with a knife. When your attacker relaxes his guard in front of the "inept victim," you can launch into him with your true capabilities.

Historically, the juxtapositioning of falsehood and reality was often used by Japanese ninja in escape tactics. A ninja might throw a heavy stone into a moat or a river and then hide in nearby foliage to trick those seeking him into searching the ripples of the water. A ninja might rush up to a group of castle guards with a frenzied tale of some calamity behind him. As the guards rush off, the ninja could slip through the gate to go and "warn" other guards, while making his escape instead.

The pretense of innocence, or the appearance of being offguard or not suspecting, is also a way of using the deception strategy. Traitors within an organization might be allowed to remain, and they might be supplied with false information to confuse the enemy. The appearance of a castle or camp unprepared for war could be a trap to lure the enemy into attacking against superior numbers. Perhaps the most universal and fundamental application of this innocent deception was the anonymity of the historical ninja. The ninja had a cover occupation and family, and if he were successful, no one ever learned that he was in truth a ninja agent.

In its truest form, the way of ninjutsu is the way of *in shin tonkei,* which can be paraphrased as the contemporary "accomplishing the most with the least amount of effort," or winning and obtaining the desired results while interfering with the natural order of things in the smallest degree possible. A general characteristic of ninjutsu is the tendency to rely on *in,* or negative and dark, escapes and battle plans when dealing with adversity or opposition. Whenever presented with a choice between a battle or subterfuge, the ninja relies on the more passive deceptive strategy. When choosing between conquering an adversary's will or guiding his thinking, the ninja prefers to assist the adversary in wanting to see things the ninja's way. Unhindered by rigid codes of honor that could force other men into suicidal actions despite their own better judgement, the ninja is free to employ his common sense in order to accomplish his objectives while eliminating personal danger. For the unenlightened observer, this method often creates the impression that the ninja has given up his ideals or surrendered, while his true intentions and the actual desired prize are kept well-concealed or disguised. By relying more on the *in* approach, the ninja reduces the discernability of his influence on the situation, and thereby reduces his vulnerability at the hands of those who would retaliate or hold him responsible for unforeseen occurrences. The ninja's motto of "no name and no art" works to prevent him from unknowingly making a target out of himself, and it keeps him out of the sights of those who would not wish him well.

The ninja's *in* approach to living, which followed the ways of nature, was in dramatic contrast to the bold *yo* philosophies of the samurai warrior class. The way of the samurai was said to be the way of death, and the true samurai structured his life in preparation for the moment of his death. To die in fierce combat in service to his lord was said to be the ultimate purpose or achievement of the samurai life, and an exquisite death was the desired prize. The social order, the proprieties, a strong sense of justice and moral right, complete dedication to a ruler, and the almost stylized refinement of the emotions characterized the height of the samurai culture.

The ninja was looked down upon with contempt and disgust by the samurai, and, indeed, the ninja's responsive, naturalistic in shin tonkei outlook appears to be a disordered, prideless, rowdy, and perhaps even cowardly life when compared to the structured dignity of the samurai. The historical ninja was only as loyal as the moment demanded, fighting for the rulers of the day who condoned the ninja's life ideals. The ninja observed no social structure or priorities, and, except for belonging to a loosely formed clan, possessed no family name or history in the community whatsoever. Guided by their mystical philosophies of the balancing *in* and *yo* interaction among the elements of nature, the ninja acknowledged no absolute concept of justice, fairness, or morality, and held in their hearts the knowledge that the vast universe would continue to unfold with the beauty of impersonal totality that knows no right or wrong.

The samurai was guided by external considerations. The method or form used to accomplish something often became more important than the final outcome itself. This philosophy dictated that the way one appears is the only reality, and that one concentrates on the details of speech and action in order to develop the heart and spirit. If one appears foolish, one is foolish. If one appears weak, then one certainly is weak. If one appears to be an immoral coward, then one is an immoral coward. This tradition of bold *yo* manliness is reflected today in the training of many of the contemporary Oriental martial arts. Unlike ninjutsu, power is worshiped in these martial arts, loyalty is rewarded, discipline is expected, and dynamic action is seen to be the only key to handling any crisis.

The martial art of ninjutsu does have its strong *yo* elements; however, the system also includes a wide-ranging scope of alternate *in* approaches to life's conflicts. Internal considerations shape external reality from the heart and spirit, and life becomes a reflection of our beliefs. The results outweigh the means in the final analysis. The truth is held in the heart, the personality sees with more than the eyes alone, and the external elements become our tools, or toys, for use in the fulfillment of our soul's intentions.

The world continues to spin into days and nights, winters and springs, and we can accept, understand, and relish the experience, or dissipate ourselves by resisting and demanding that the universe conform to the small scale ignorance of some rigid creed or list of beliefs. This is the ultimate joyous lesson to be learned, the total freedom that formed the ninja shadow warrior's code of life, and expanded into the tenets of the philosophy of ninjutsu—the way of winning naturally through the art of understanding. ∎